SNOW DANCING
WITH THE
AURIUM
OF THE
FALLS

Second Edition

SNOW DANCING

WITH THE

AURIUM

OF THE

FALLS

Poems for The Tiny Village Intention

by Jane Engleman

Second Edition

> *Aurium is the latin plural of auris, the ear.*
> *We dance gently driven with listening waters the melody of spring melt.*
> *This is how we know each other.*
> *This is how we love us together unself-consciously.*

Snow Dancing with the Aurium of the Falls
Copyright © 2024 by Jane Engleman
ISBN: 979-8-218-37083-1

Second Edition

Highland Park, CA 90042

Cover Design: Heidi Unkefer

Layout Design: Jane Engleman & Emily Anne Evans

*To those who leave the locks off the doors
and windows in community spaces,
and to those with enough hope and courage
to allow them to be left open:*

Kerry Morrison & Heart Forward LA

Fountain House Hollywood Clubhouse

Fred Sugerman & Colleen Sugerman, Medicine Dance

NonPerformance Workshops NonPerformance
Race Relay
Tuesday Dance Studio

Hiram Sims & the 2022 Class of Cal State LA

Sims Library of Poetry
Community Literature Initiative

Gustavo Dudamel

The L.A. Philharmonic
Youth Orchestra of Los Angeles

Table of Contents

SECTION TWO: Antelopes

SECTION FIVE: Birds

SECTION SIX: Wild Horses

SECTION SEVEN: Bees

Acknowledgments

I have so many to acknowledge.
It would take the Library of Congress
and the Rock Writing in the Canyons.

But I want to thank today my community
that has kept me alive since recovery:

Olga Peralta

my mentor, my friend and my Black Antelope

Sylvia Rodriquez

my sacred fifth mother, my medicine woman

Daniel Campos

my teacher, the lion warrior who inspires me to go on, go on...

<u>Preface</u>

<u>*To My Dance Coach*</u>

We run too fast to see the trees are dancing, the birds are singing,
the flowers and winds are painting. We rest stop only long enough to
shoot the buffalo, the elk, the antelope and the Indians; and when the
world turns against us, we build forts, bays, cubicles and "treatment
centers." We slaughter everything on the road-trip to heaven and
eternal life. We own our own prisons, closets and cattle chutes.

Never learning what to do with bare hands and pure hearts, we are
denied the universe, which is out there, in here, inviting, waiting.

A book, my life, is not a formality but an accident of windshift,

a note on a scrap we found dancing along the asphalt. It feels crazy to
me I ever wrote anything before I danced. It feels crazy to me I could
have been a poet before I lived, before I began to listen.

Maestro, you teach us all to breathe to wait to move, to feel to flow
into the brief flash of performance. "There is plenty of time to dance,"
you say, "in the last few moments."

We were all laughing together on a Tuesday when we noticed a
wonderful song scribbled in pencil on a napkin in the asphalt of that
pretty stone church. The whole parking lot is littered with incremental
melt like syllable snowflakes. The singers might still be out there
nestled in goose down

with blue bunches of free tickets for hot dogs

- and little red ukuleles –

in the hollows in the hedges by the bus stop.

SNOW DANCING

WITH THE

AURIUM

OF THE

FALLS

INTRO: The Gate at the Bridge

<u>Light</u>

As a laser, a light is not easy,
and it is not lazy;
it cuts, it burns,
it closes down color
like a cauterized clam,

sometimes for a long
long time.

Vulnerability illuminates the agony
that love cannot break out of a prism
without
difference/division...

Let it go

Light refracts

Little Yellow Dog

The little yellow dog was wounded, broken, bit up, beat and a little soggy, saggy,
ran into the wrong dog
and the wrong man with a bat, her long yellow ears torn up in tuffs
of soggy bloody squealing, shocked sideways, long tail tucked, squeezed flat
dragged under the trailer park chain link fence
and just started running, shoulder kind of hanging down running in a running
easy as the man and the big dog couldn't get through, the jolt
of the cool blew on her cuts, the bites, to feel
a little better, but bones of her hip ground down heft like broken, but not broken
bad, only pulled or yanked, but they'd got the puppies.

The puppies were gone.

They'd got the puppies, the puppies were gone, but she couldn't think
about that, running in an alley down
the bank of cement, running in cool wind up over a pile of rags, dirt oil, and cans and glass,
they'd got the puppies, but she couldn't think
about that, head beginning to flash, beat-hot to throb, she came up
over a knob beside the asphalt up a curvy dirt road, litter
of white rock and green scruff up between the tar of a telephone pole
to a wreck of a blue car,
the door buried open; she crawled in
to dawn in copper architecture in myth, wires and towers in the real old leather
of a rent seat, passenger side, safe, good in a bed half-hill and
half-wreck, windshield intact to hold off the cold in the morning, solid steel
gray metal of ceiling and crack of an open exit in the back seat. They'd got the puppies,

the puppies were gone,

but she couldn't think about that, she finally began to lick her wounds, to lick, to lick
to whine

to soften.

Six Old Friends

There are six of us old friends, old funky fighters,
up by the Ponderosa bridge.
We live in holes and crevices, floors of clay lit by windows of wood
or the tiny fires in a cairn of rock. For lack
of better names, we are called
Earth, Fire, Wind, Water, Space and Consciousness;
never Wise alone, and never wise
without a question. We wait by the bridge,
sometimes snow dancing with the aurium of the falls.

The children play in the shadows of the pools,
slow gliding cool glass flickering down beside us.
Sometimes the young ladies come to ask a thing;
we take turns holding nervous fingers;
we take turns slobber-kissing babies.
We love the lonely, encouraging the independent.

Sometimes men come around, young men, strong wrinkled men come,
sweaty and hungry and angry and we feed them
a little corn, a little joke, a little fresh-cracked bread.
We take a little time to rub their shoulders, sending them off
to the heat of the workshops, offices, the fields.

Different ones come by, we take turns to hear them
appreciate themselves, falling crazy in love
with their way of knowing things.

Strangers come by
having accidently hiked five-hundred miles
up into the mountains,
and we together chatter them up, watching,
until they want to get back down.

We're always here.
　　We always have been.
　　　　Whoever comes here,
　　　　　　　　we're here to listen, to tell the myths and metaphors,
　　　　　　make sense of the science, to laugh at with them
and cry all together in a chorus when it comes.

　　　　Fire crackles
　　　　with the wishing of the Water and sometimes
　　　　Space says nothing.
　　　　　　　　　Until You listen, You cannot hear;
　　　　　　　until You look, You cannot see
　　　　　　there is nothing and everything here;
　　　　"Play what is not there."
　　　　Wind cheerily moans to the sound of the ground
　　　　of the Earth turning slowly to paint and carve.
　　　　　　　　See her, know her...
　　　　Consciousness moves us alive. We are then so.
　　　　　　　　　　Alive.

Something magic happens in the mercy of communion.
　　　　　Some healing, some peace.
　　　　　Some fun, some desire,
　　　　　some tools, some understanding
　　　　　　　　　for anyone present.

Why, if we are not sat with, we do not offer.
　　　　　　We never push, we wait
　　　　but sometimes some find it good to seek, and find to satisfaction.
　　　　　　　　Just takes dance and time.
　　　　　It's not a book really.
　　　　　　　　Just a long, long, long, long
　　　　　raucous quiet rhyme.

Drowning of the Goddesses

"I am not my mother, but I know her pretty good.
The trick is to come to love her."

I fell into the river that saved me. It roared
and it plunged underground.
Oshun was in the water, and Lofn, Pachamama. Aphrodite was in the water...
White Shell Woman, Isis, Xochiquetzal, Mother Mary, Yue Lao, all of them
were flailing in the water.
Millions of goddesses were in the caves along with the guy that hurt me, so bad.
We wouldn't be dancing together in the waves.
I was alone.
It was busy.

We decided not to teach hope
anymore. We were carrying by force. Time went lost. We were always so, so cold. We decided
not to teach time
in the fury. We forgot together
to move.
I was desolate. We were screaming
without a Voice in the violence.

We decided to worship the war.
We decided to teach shock and isolation.
We decided not to rock our babies, teach life
to our grandchildren anymore. We forgot their possibilities. We forgot to enjoy their liveliness.
We were hit with switches and beaten with rocks. There was no time to talk.
I was alone, curled in Pain.
We decided to get used to it, heaving and choking in dirty running and rioting
and branches and water and water and blood, filibuster and freezing old bark.

We decided not to teach patient companionship and
mindful sensuality on a date anymore. It was unnecessary.

Deaf must mean there is nothing to be heard.
No light meant there was nothing to see.

We decided not to teach courage anymore. We couldn't believe it. We had cold shoulders
and battered lips.
We just decided to teach terror and fear. It was all there was
in there. The pitch of the river rose and darkened.
The centuries passed unbalanced by
meaning or words. My thighs and belly were torn with wounds forever.
There was no time in all that time for CBT, for DBT.
It was prolonged. It didn't stop with treatment. We were unable to think.
I could not apprehend strong gentle fingers. Only the lashing of cold.

We forgot about loudly teaching love together softly
anymore. We were lost. Our grandchildren were lost.
I was lost. Sick. Dizzy. Abandoned.
Suddenly you held the arms of my child,
heaving and crying and yanking back.
Are we not all birthed in Water, in Spirit, bloody, washed, free, ugly and small?
We dragged up on the bank on our stomachs, face down on the ground.
Throw a blanket around my shaking, hold me in Daisy Taugelchee's beautiful design.
Slather on the Tiger Balm. Slide in the needle. Wrap us in the bear hug of Yoki Saito's quilts,
with beauty surrounding us, in the height and breadth of the depth
of the Love of the One I Am.
We are waking, Mother; I am waking up.
Hand me our children, our warriors and workers.
Lead me, like Mother Moses,
to get them out of there.
Teach me the patience of an Inuit aunty. Offer Sacraments and Strudel.
Bring our grandmothers back. Make my broken mother warm.
Twist our freezing fingers on Mayan Chocolate.
Let us look and feel and know
this sky, this wind, this breath, the cold beauty of dawn.
I have decided, we have decided to teach
with these blue shivering blue lips all that has been spoken.

Wall

"Don't play what's there, play what's not there." —Miles Davis

"An empty canvas is full." —Robert Rauschenberg

This lady got this wall that she bought. No door, no window, no lock.
    She could put in
        a counter for a crockpot full of chicken soup. Why not? Not this
          lady busy making something of it.
              She could always go out,
        but she rocks and she knocks at the sheetrock. Her wall.

    Her wall. Her wall. Her wall.
           Paint cans, Mod Podge, graffiti and gauze, the call
  of the wall for a nurse or a priest
          or a pill for dirty dishes
          or dirty wishes and six broken whiskey bottles.

TRUTH IS A TRIP. So she projects herself
     into the scream that memes the illuminated dreams
       where the smelly of the sewers don't stink
         in this snowy kitchenette of mahogany rock gonna "Ring!"
     gonna "Sing!" like only water gongs go in a spring of Sangria for those
          who like murals of Revolution.

And you can't break a nut of fanatic devotion!
      The clocks are talking trash.
         Her back's to the moon,
    Her back's to the comforter;
         Her back's to the cup of cold... What?
    She can't see the stack of taxes, or the can of pork and beans.

Walls are fixed white by lies and laws, and in-laws,...
when, in fact, a pretty pony could make it all stop,
                                but you can't tell the scribble from the face,
                the tattoo, the napkin or the Mac.

                Sanity don't track without the re-edit, the edit, the edit, the
re-organize!

                                Paint! Pain! The epic. The pall of the unfinished WALL.
                Pixels on a piece of Sheetrock after all...

Aesthetics simply couldn't be The Great Wall,
                an old lady on her scrappy knees
                                frantic to conceal it
                                                or dress it up pretty and please?
                And who, or What, says "Done?" All I see is a high wall!
                                HEY... WALL!
                Heh...
        Hi, Wall.
        My wall.

<u>*Shine*</u>

Make say your lines while the lights shine,
      the curtain part to brilliance coming stumbling through in a
            bloody shower
      in a puddle of floody light and action
   tumbling the drumsoul of a wood stage struck by enlightening here in the
middle,

            nearly, dearly, accidental...

    You got one hour,
      in the hole in the hold of omnificence
and we don't know it. Characters and caricatures on broken legs
           and foreigners, worked
        out
        in scripts of hightech chipchirp.

     I just thought it was me,
   but there ain't no queen without the crown, the palace or pageant,
    no dean without a peer review in a quad 'n a class;
     no nobles or fairies or contra sopranos
       with no grapes for the wine,
    wheat for the wafers,
      muscle and the will of designers and gaffers.
 "The Wiz"'ll play on without us.

We have this spotlight splishsplash
     beam in the billowhollow see for an hour
         a part in the stormsong starfall of
    audience of one, restive, and coughing,
      holding your breath for love
        of a moment changing
    in the wings because of it.

We Thought They Took Our Souls

We thought they took our souls, but they didn't, but we thought so.
So they came on down the mountains through the passes, a beast,
a many-colored dragon, driving
their horses, their elephants, flags, panzers, papers, helicopters,
howitzers, cruisers and scientific omniscience over upon us,
armored steeds and ships and statistics, weapons
of mass, mass, mass, mass destruction:
and we lit
out of the ceremony
of singing and the dancing.
We scattered
and ran for our lives.
We thought they took our souls, but they didn't, but we thought so.
They wanted the life we had itself.
Our villages. Our cuisine.
Our poetry and animals.
Our painted crafts.
They wanted the love they would never kneel to acknowledge, yet isolated
us
in cubicles, cars, dotplots, gridlock;
took us down
One
by
one
by
1
:
.

Fractals Buried in Seeds

(in a Little Pot in a Ruin)

Gold scars in bone china vaults, they wait…
Choctaw baskets, Scottish cauldrons, Dia de Los Muertos,
The Beauty Way, the Book of Mary,
the blue scarab, the ruby-throated hummingbird, they wait…

Scraps of dirty maps whispering back a Red Sea
through the underground railroad,
abandoned asylums and silver mines,
brick potato cellars, herbal medicines in Bell jars,
trunks and sanctuary under hand-maid rugs, they wait…
libraries in sandstone, towering sign languages on ballads of rock,
spiraling calligraphy of condors
circling stories in the embers of elders, they wait…
Pipes of peace, rockets, they smoke and they wait…

The Great Soul rises. Polyamory
of science, art, sex and mystery, whispers in Sage
silent surrender to the thunder of the underpasses,
drumming fossil rhododendron dancing, drunken,
rocked by maestras who watch, they wait…

Swelling like blueberries and bears,
babushkas in radiant projects, honeycombs of carcasses,
uranium, lightning, lioness, they wait,
steel, back bone connected to the witch moon
screaming in labor, they ride, finally free
and flowing like pilgrim ships,
wolves, ash, choice and snow flakes pouring
across the flaming horizon.

Consternation of the Bees

"Colony Collapse Disorder is the phenomenon that occurs when the majority of worker bees in a colony disappear and leave behind a queen, plenty of food and a few nurse bees to care for the remaining immature bees and the queen. Once thought to pose a major long term threat to bees, reported cases of CCD have declined substantially over the last five years."[1]

I love science and history. And I guess I hate science and history. Mental illness is in every twist and turn of my science and history, embedded in my DNA, in my family, in my culture and in my country. But I read because not only do they give me the bad and the ugly, they also provide understanding of cycles of weather patterns, cycles of imperialism and power, cycles of seasons and cycles of generations. It gives me patience. It makes me laugh at the way we see other cultures and other lifeforms. It gives me ancient blueprints and guides. Ann Lamont says, "How do we celebrate paradox, let alone manage it all? ... We remember mustard seeds, that the littlest things will have great results. We do the smallest, realest, most human things. **We water what is dry.**"[2]

The colony of Los Angeles has collapsed. If you do not see it, you are living in a virtual reality staring into a carefully spun screen rather than out the open windows. You do not hear the silence, you do not smell the stench and you do not notice the empty rooms. The Environmental Protection Agency says that when a bee hive develops Colony Collapse Disorder, there may be several reasons, such as "disease," "pesticide poisoning," "stress due to management practices such as transportation to multiple locations across the country for providing pollination services," "changes to the habitat," "inadequate forage/poor nutrition," and "potential immune-suppressing stress on bees."

This is not an essay on bees, but I am seeing parallels to the collapse of intentional communities in the tattered thrift-store remnants of the British Empire in California. California is the last edge of the new world. The refugees of New England are settled here. We have no place else to go.

---

1   https://www.epa.gov/pollinator-protection/colony-collapse-disorder

2   https://datebook.sfchronicle.com/books/review-almost-everything-notes-on-hope-by-anne-lamott
https://shelf-awareness.com/issue.html?issue=3340#m41904
Almost Everything: Notes on Hope by Anne Lamott (Riverhead, $20 hardcover, 208p., 9780525537441, October 16, 2018)

<u>Self-Care in Colony Collapse Disorder</u>

From 1988 to 2013, I struggled with severe mental illness. As a missionary kid in New Mexico, I was shamed, confused, enraged and terrified, caught between neglect, violence and the paradoxes of what I know to be true in one culture and what I know to be true in another. I was given free hope and some community support in the board and care home provided by Homes for Life Foundation, and in the I-CAN program in Pasadena which became a Community Mental Health Center under the Department of Mental Health. If I had not had these, I would be dead, sacked out on illegal drugs in a tent on Skid Row or in jail, three outcomes which some in our society seem to believe can only be "managed" by forced assimilation through education, economic sanction, withholding primary healthcare, or even "scientific" euthanization of the "useless eaters."

Killing or mechanizing bees and humans bees is not sustainable. Everything is connected to the flow of abundance. Killing ourselves through stress is not the answer, nor is living with walking corpses who are becoming desperately violent on every corner. But how do we manage paradox, let alone manage it all? Or like Rumi we can ask how to get back to that place where birds know how to nest?

While in twenty-five years in community mental health, the L.A. Department of Mental Health marketed at great expense the concept of "Recovery." I found I-CAN after nine years doing everything possible to navigate society and my own confusion. I was in abject hopelessness, at zero resource. My family was at zero resource. I had no community. So I latched on to this concept of "Recovery," and came to worship the idea that if I continued to be "compliant," took "scientific" drugs approved by the FDA and squeezed into the tiny square box insisted upon in behavioral mental health treatment in the united States, I would come to that nirvana of "Recovery." If I sat in my chair in a support group long enough, life would re-emerge.

Some practices remind me of Richard Henry Pratt's attempts at the Carlyle Indian School: "Kill the Indian, save the man."[3] And when the experiment fails (when you find you cannot make a milk cow out of a honey bee), the statistics show that *bees* are useless. This substitute for science descends into insanity, a result of the arrogance of limited perspective; if the scientist, Isaac Newton, in the 1600s had found an uncharged cellphone by his bed, he might have collected it as an art object or stuck it in a box for future reference. The technology would have been useless to him disconnected from a tutorial or a wifi tower,

---

3   Gene Demby. The Ugly, Fascinating History Of The Word 'Racism'. NPR.org. January 6, 2014. Accessed November 11, 2016.

and how ridiculous he would have come across in a Freshman college class in 2022. Empirical science is in its infancy in social work.

Science is only as good as the innate work of the bees; whether or not you understand what you are looking at, you will find out why they are essential, one way or the other. And community systems have not been permitted in the united States. Education is focused on masculine projects. Civilizations collapse without intact communities and, by the way, villages cannot be sustained without the independent business networking of mothers. Women are natural community builders when respected, supported and left to our own devices. Educating a workforce includes more than an assembly of lines, cubicles and paperwork.

The Science of Community

Since 1917, when Mississippi became the last state to pass compulsory education, we have been given "the American dream."[4] And in mental health, we were given grand examples of the diagnoses of great European and American leaders who had suffered and risen to greatness. These great leaders are not the leaders who lived in hogans in the desert, nor were they the mothers of the black and white politicians, scientists and artists who raised them.

When I began my journey, I believed that I could become strong enough to contribute to my country. Then I thought perhaps I could save my family. And then I came to believe that the only person I could ever rescue was myself. I was wrong. When colonies collapse, the bees are at the mercy of something outside themselves.

We cannot DO self-care when our environment has become poisoned by the seven sins, and only the rich believe they have the means to escape. I guess they could build giant air-rockets and transport "the bees" off to Titan to let the planet recover, as the British did with their poor and criminalized, shipping "prostitutes" and "murderers" to America and Australia, but finally, are the British better people having purified the problem?

The State has chosen to deport or oppress our workers, refusing citizenship to many, making debtors and slaves of the college students bred to be our nobles, doctors and Brahmans. The contamination of

---

4   "Mississippi was the last state to pass a law requiring school attendance in 1917. Still, enforcement of these state laws was largely ineffective until states began to realize the value of an educated workforce." https://www.findlaw.com/education/education-options/compulsory-education-laws-background.html

eugenics in "behavioral mental health" has created an epidemic of anosognosia in the united States. Now the assimilated can decide which cultures, genders and thinkers are insane and how they should be "managed." Researchers are deaf to the voices of history, geography and all voices not transmitted through established digital frequencies. "Special Ed" is the State solution for neurodiversity or difference. Unassimilated mothers do not teach the courses on the observed psychology of children from the perspectives of their own languages and cultures.

And so, clients are beaten, forgotten, psychologically tortured, isolated, fingerprinted, drugged and finally "put to bed." And so the endless search for "more beds," in jails, convalescent homes, "tiny house villages," tool sheds on the freeways and beautiful new apartment complexes micromanaged and locked in after 5 pm.

How do we get back to the place where bees know how to hive, where unstressed mothers teach each other to breastfeed, stop and rock and to discipline gently? Where artists are heard? I would ask if corporate scientists are temperamentally capable of accessing sensory input beyond what they see in front of their physical eyes?

More Quotes On Bees:

- "Where would we be without bees? As far as important species go, they are top of the list. They are critical pollinators."[5]

- "If delicate flowers are to turn into succulent fruits, they need the help of honey bees. Eighty percent of all fruit and vegetable varieties rely on insect pollination."[6]

- "Bees contribute to complex, interconnected ecosystems that allow a diverse number of different species to co-exist."[7]

How To Get Back To That Place Where Birds Know How To Nest?

I never used to think of writing as hard work, or even necessary. Nor, after years of labeling (by white male psychiatrists with no understanding of art, of the feminine principle or of indigenous wisdom) did

---

5 https://www.bbc.com/future/article/20140502-what-if-bees-went-extinct

6 https://www.britannica.com/video/179537/colony-collapse-disorder

7 https://www.actionnews5.com/2021/05/19/breakdown-why-bees-are-important-environment/

I ever imagine that I have a reason to exist or that I could have a gift, that of beeing; I spend my days playing in the petals and pooping in the hive. I am a worker bee, and I am dying too. Death is a gift of urgency and energy with the beautiful peace of knowing that you are disabled and able to work in a flow in teams

Animals and plants teach us how our teeny weeny individual strengths and innate wisdom contribute to the well-being at least of this continent, if not the world, if not the rest of space. I cannot be an activist in Los Angeles. I can only bee. Part of the beeing is sitting with Creativity who calls me gently to the network of restoration of independent intentional communities in Los Angeles.

Heart Forward LA is a restoration project for human intentional communities in Los Angeles. The Clubhouse model is focused on those diagnosed by State criteria, but it a model of the ancient and the contemporary movement to restore urban connected villages where seniors and the disabled, the orphans of insanity, workers, pets, plants,and children can *dwell* together again. It is a pilot that can be replicated. If it can be done at the last seam of emigration on the planet, within twenty miles of the beach, with the most, most marginalized, it can be done anywhere. A clubhouse. A meeting place. The beginning of village. It won't look like what we think. It will look like what we dance in time.

I end with the quote by the EPA with which I began: ***"Once thought to pose a major long term threat to bees, reported cases of CCD have declined substantially over the last five years."***[8] Who knows why? Perhaps the pandemic has made an impact on Colony Collapse Disorder, or restoration has been made by some natural cycle of weather or planetary tilt, or maybe bees are returning because of continuing teamwork among bees, beekeepers, scientists and connoisseurs who love their honey?

---

8   https://www.epa.gov/pollinator-protection/colony-collapse-disorder

Rain of the Feminine (First)

They teach us to move.
They lead us to want. They teach us to move in the rain
and thunder.

They teach us to play in the dance of the rain
loving along down the sides of the cliffs
in swirls in the washes, to run
in the water with caked bare feet, scrambling over the rocks,
toes so caked in clay
the cactus doesn't even matter, our faces
massaged by the oil of the sky, our eyes streaming light, rocked easy
in the clouds with the warm fat skirts,
feeling again while watching everybody else
while looking at all the mountains. They teach us to dance in the
female rain.

A Letter to Water

"Paarame Xaa, I Thirst" (Tongva)

I am writing to You, thanking You for coming to save my life when there was nowhere left for me to go. You took me down to the deep waters in the rock, the black crystal thunder of Your loving Soul. You spent Time with me when I could not spend the time with You; there was too much. Terror. Unsafety. Things to do.

Thank You, Thee, They, Them, for the carnival ride through echoing caverns in the bulky rocking of a cradle, through the star-story splash of sparks and metal light in an opera of moving rock wiring, hieroglyphs and sand-salt space. I heard you, barely, through the wound before You introduced me to the Wind. You whispered sound across my naked ears, shockingly refreshing, warm with Breath. You are Darkness and Dawn. I was carried away.

When I first saw what is gold in the stonecloud horizon, I saw myself I as an orphan, just sliding up the sash of a hermitage in Shigaraki Village. You told me, wordless to go on. You flowed in me, with me. The giant cradle jerked me spinning down in a shriek of spray; You held me like an auntie through the graphic jet of the Milky Way. You shouted and laughed with the adventure. Oh, I screamed and cried, shook and balked, tried to climb over the side, but you grabbed me by the waist and held me. "There is no way but through the ride, Child, no shore, no lifeboat, no hospital ship. You simply learn to love it."

In all that time, I never knew You, never recognized Your face. You simply called me to listen. You are madonna, whale, eagle and the university, personal and impersonal, old African storyteller and golden princess, Zuni warrior, Vietnamese guerilla mother and Thomas Paine. You spoke with languages that had no lexicon, no dictionary with abridgement, before the civil, the Babel, in that ocean of beings who feel the currents, where the waters fall and ride to gravity into the laughing pool.

You opened to the delta, and let me go on. The troubled voyage is an invitation to explore new worlds, not to conquer but enjoy. So You opened your mouth and I speak. So how can I be ever afraid? We open our mouth to use our mouth in dance and surgery. With You, I speak. Presently.

SECTION ONE: Bobcat

<u>Ranger</u>

This morning I found a Bobcat
hissing from her den,
dragged out by the ranger
to take my medicine.

That ranger's a stranger, after all, he'd
have to be mad to save me, growling
and soggy and spitting and ears torn back.

Maybe everybody else does better in herds
and flocks than in the gloomy shadows
with my raggedy pile of skinny fuzzy drippy
kits, but I got sharp claws,
great teeth and an expensive hide,
with a larger range of wandering wary
and independent in places most people
wouldn't ever go there
until chased and trapped.

Flat Horizon

You do not want
to begin. The desert breathes.
The desert dances.
It enlivens you. You cannot
know what will happen.
You don't want to go there.
And you do not know Them
really. You met them once.
You loved them; they were attractive,
and brilliant,
and funny and effective.
But what if they were
who you did not think they were
or who you did not want
them to be? Don't bother going over.
But you know you are. You kind of have to.
Sharon Hawley on a lone dreamtrek
bikeabout. Orozco on a white wall.
Hiram Sims in a kindergarten
before the opening of the Conference.
It is not you moving; it is
the universe heaving over like a fat
lady and there is only so much
tip you can take; you're going over.
You find the ice crust,
the waffle stompers
and the setting moon
sublime. Trinity.

Assimilation

One year after the war began
and ninety-five after the Declaration of Independence,
Abraham Lincoln had us arrested for stealing
a bunch of horses from the guy who stole our ranch.

We took off down our alley, like we always did,
but they got us, caught us, hauled us off to the County Jail.
"I will never steal another horse."

We couldn't make bail.
We couldn't afford a two-bit lawyer.
And they cut our hair off, you know,
the rain, you know, the long wise life of rain.

They sure didn't want us speaking the language of Diné Bizaad.
Threatened their sense of omniscience.
I went crazy and kicked a guard; they threw
me down in solitary. They made me take these pills;
big white pills in a little paper cup to shut me up.
"I will never steal another horse."

Actually, after a while,
you sure get to like those pills, only
I kinda think them pills for depression
would work a little better with a cure for oppression…

Anyways, they kept us locked up in there about a hundred and fifty-four years, you know.
We were in those walls so long; I mean, we forgot
who we even were. I couldn't remember
what my mother looked like.
We forgot how the sun feels,
you know, the wind… (swoosh).

One day, an attorney came in. You know,
                    "I will never steal another horse!"
          I wrote that 500 times on the walls, on the papers:
                    "I will never steal another horse."

          Well, they let us go home.
They even let us live two hundred miles next door to our grandmothers' house,
                    long as we paid the rent.
          No water, no rivers to run dry and mess up a treaty, but hey...
                    "Oh, hey, Preacher! Ya'ahteeh!"...
                              ..."Yeah, maybe I'll come this Sunday...."

     ..."Yeah, hey, Mrs. White, are you still teaching English?...
          ...Yeah, I'll sure come back to college next year...
          ...Yeah, you take it easy! See ya."...
                              You kidding me? You know, don't stick your infected
                    American drive into my native operating system!

Last time they dragged me off to school, they tried to teach me about
                              how to get in debt to a white man.
                    I already know how to get in debt;
                              You just steal a bunch of
                                        horses
                    off your own ranch.
     You know, and I don't need to steal no horses; You know, Man,
                    my cousin just bought us another thoroughbred;
          we got thoroughbreds, paints and appaloosas. Yeah,
                    he's got me riding again.
          I get up at 4:30 every morning and ride
horses all day as fast as they can run! I walk in Beauty!
                    I ride in Beauty.
                              Together we ride!

Bullet

"Souls grow slow; why'd you want to go down that rabbit hole?
You don't even dream what's down there."

It's three o'clock.
        You haven't moved, screens blinking, from where you puffed three quarters
          of the day.
            What will you do if she doesn't make it in to wipe the poop off
the laminate or pay the gas, what happens if you're sick
               and can't get to the food bank?

       Living takes
   money. If you had money, you'd have a reason to live. If you had a train to go across
the country, you'd have reason...
         Listening is costly. Speak American. Then we'll know what you need,
and I know how to get it. Money is a living;
        we live, money moves, money comes up "sweet"...
     in any language.
       The lines are all connected,
         fettuccini; we run our own trains... I own the mechanics;
           we own the windows, the carpet
  you're thrown on. We'll throw, just like we always done, forth heat
       and currency until the damn
              little banana bread dining car sweats gold.

       Money should be God.
        We should have lots.
      You get up enough, you might could have some...
        Tweeeeeeet! Tweeeeeeeet!

Layovers are unacceptable. Sitting's too much. I should...
tell you what to do and you should... help yourself.

Waste is one hundred and eighty-two sleeping browsers
functioning at the data chip,
failing to get anybody to Chicago. I got the comprehensive
protocol, we don't need the unction...
It's quick on the metal track, swiftly up from the carrier,
unifying school children into platforms, evading public flack, zipping suit cases
over civil graces,
making it a crime of not swigging diesel, gnawing every little crumb of platinum—
to try to get up and shower, and change into a dress...
You should donate, you! Yes. Fascism is cheap, friendly and quick.
My money's easy; my burden is thick! And greed is extremely expensive!

And what is it you got in the end? I'm showing you,
I'm getting you on track! Now, I've got to run... run!
Run! RUN! ...
I'll get you to the church,
I'll get you to the Bachelor's,
I'll get you to the crowning between your legs,
I'll get you to retirement and beyond, and
I'll get you there on time... After that?
After that? Well science doesn't show there any
life there, after.
Look at the money. And what have you got there, honey? A ticket!
I don't know about you
but I'm on the clock!
We just get to go through...What?

Depression Arrythmia

Open up, Heart, in labyrinths of sheetrock,
marbline spiraling artwork, the electric mind,
the shocking horizon.
The arts are the eyes,
the poems ears,
the voice of the body in mind.
How can we think without the color of our skin?
Open them, or close them to see, hear, love. Hold until you notice.
The world is too weary, too jade
to get up again now, after all these tribulations,
will not set a foot on the ground,
will not pull the curtain, or face the window.
Hold until you move. Stop until you find.
Open your mind. Dance barefoot in April
across the campus path between the sidewalks.

We cannot move
or love, and why?,
without sense. I love you with music.
I hear you the wind. I feel the feeling in bone-ache and glory.
I am loving each of you now in poems.

No sense is nonsense.
One sense is blind sense.
"I think, therefore I am"?
(I love you now. I love you in my fingers.)
I *feel*,
therefore I can.

Thirty-Year Mortgage, Amortized

"If you won't consent to be a pet in the cage you rent,
we'll provide a convincing habitat in the billion-dollar county zoo."

'nuff already. 'nuff! Enough!
Is the Creator so miserly we gotta a marry ourselves
for thirty years to a changing stranger
who complains about having to look up our names?
You can tell the principals
in management consulting, hard and starving, mean, lean and hungry.
Time is a lender with an appetite for molé and the saxaphone.
Mercy allows for harm reduction
Take the crack, vodka, debting,
porn, prisons, politics and stubborn isolation,
overwork, law and underlearning, your cutting, your war...
gifts as you need them as a coping skill until you find the real.
Caring hangs out in the kitchen with cornbread and kindness
to serve you hot in bowls of clay.
Your first lesson
will be cold, cold, cold spring water with a squirt of lemon.
Wash your hands and sit. Come meet my Blinky, Kinky, Minky and Stinky;
four senior members of a many-step support group
who give more from a college fish tank than a banker.
Go on and swim, shimmering
sway, just because you are human.
Wisdom is that Person giving us a minute.
Please come home. 'nuff already. Enough.
'nuff, 'nuff, 'NUFF! We can always live together.
Wealth in this living room is compounded daily.
Everything else is
interest.

Cars

Driving is a good thing.
Long gray ways through desert, emerald hairpins up the mountain.
Driving is a good thing, but
I don't want to be driving anymore,
negotiating the centimeter past the scratch of the mailbox or watch out
for the puppies. I don't want to snap to finger the Mercedes Benz
flying low at a mile a stop with the rest of forty million stressors on the 405.
Its good to get there, meanwhile, safe inside, out from the sweat, the stumping
to the grate of the old hips, drizzle in a freeze . They make gated parking lots
for cars but disabled people don't get trees. Want to save the planet, want to be free,
sell your SUV. Give it to the Roma who wouldn't pay rent,
and plant trees,
out by the bus bench, please.
I feel your pain, your wheels, bucket seats, shatterproof glass, and maps
on your forty million foreheads as I sale on my little poems in the back seat of the bus,
admiring the drive as long as it is You hunting
the parking meter or the big blue "B" in the murk and dark, that Number
Seven Hundred Sixty Three, passing, passing longstring spark of electric wires through the woods,
fawns struck shock and all in the headlamps struck by trucks
over and over 'til the poor deer don't feel like crossing the road
anymore for the succulents, the deadwood sprouts, spring green new things used to seem so tasty;
I can't breathe from the fumes and the ash.
If six billion people owned a car
or two, it'd be quicker and efficient for the abled few, well, not a lot of room for Yosemite,
but you could get the reruns in black 'n white noir films on TV. But, uh,
I got my own piece of pi; when I die,
I'll send thirty six packs out to the octopi, junk debt saved on maintenance and insurance.
Retired, I s'pose you've driven five cars by now, their hubcaps and upholstery,
their empty trunks and vacant mirrors. Your religion is the universal ownership of cars.
They sync when they hit the see?

Autism Behind the Glass

I've got permission
not to see you;
you see,
I am blind.
What goes behind
the black iris meadows
of my dendrite pines?

What buzzes, what
crackles or snaps
in my noir deco rotundas,
gossiping along the
fibonacci starecases
where I sprout my succulents? Nothing
of substance, in red. Character chiffon, oranges,
statistics of flooding crowds.
An odd look.

Sometimes
it seems a good thing when
the door opens in; I see you by
the light of your shadow. I know
you
by your voice, your stance along the semi-
vertical
convergence.

Preschool in an Outhouse

In an outhouse.
    Jesus loved me up in a fright of lust,
    conceiving me to an exorcism, bearing me
    until I couldn't
    be born another minute
    to be bathed in love. And in a fit of drunken rage,

God battered the Navajo baby naked through
    a cooking fire, rippling, warping,
    cauterized and categorized me

a little criminal, I was three and it was all my fault,
    massaged sweetly in a flannel collage
    of Elijah's fire stood up in the corner
    in a cradleboard,
    pinned pudendum to crownpoint
    in a pine box of preschooler rulers,

upright and straight
    and narrow in pagan public by
    withering fingers on the trigger at
        thirty-odd-six of an old rugged cross.

The Elm Wound Hole

The elm is deep gray, cut-edged by
the same freeze that blanches the glass.

Great trees have deep roots and missing
branches. The wind has blown.
That branch is not coming back.
There is a giant hole from the giant branch.
The damage
has been done.

The wound winces back, back down, back
inside a mind deeper than the woods.
We cannot fish a tree there,
in streams devoid of love. You will have
to root your help in another source.
The branch is gone, leaving

another family curled
in the warmth,
storing seeds.

Amtrak Wreck

This is a train wreck.
Battered faces and body parts scattered
in tattered smoking cars
with banks in the pink
on fire. Fire! Fire! Sync or swim, find some whim to survive
this cubist clutter on an easel, half-buried in linen and dockers,
brain train shrieking smoking
on and on
all night long...

It is the role of the roll of the engine
to get you to the station;
the role of the roll of the caboose
to get you to the destination.
The role of the roll of the mother
to hold you;
the role of the roll of the father
to get you on your way.

It is the role of the roll of the lover
to help you find your One True Love;
the role of the roll of the EX
to help you find your One True Life.
The role of the roll of the beautiful
to bring you home;
the role of the roll of the bad and ugly
to drive you to the future;
The role of the roll of the scientist
to keep you on track;
the role of the roll of the poet
to give you the freedom to abstract.

Love is a careering locomotive of anatomy parts,
the motivational trip-up failure,
the cold unfinished shoulder, and is
the clickety clack of the keys,
the curves,
the observation car of peering
pupils streaming in a metal box
with a rhythmic beat, hugging, tugging,
chugging up the
right
track of this that art studio that buckles and bleeds
red violet black and blue
Sunset. The sacred Jet,
that Rose
in sunrise.

A Much Older Woman in Camp

I am a woman, and so my drawings will be forgotten, brushed over
in the mirror before the rush to the train.
We came through the black forest,
the nodding pines before they were cut
for masts of navies and flags of fascists,
through the beautiful needles, crooked lines of lily and ivy in fairytale books.

They'd long been taking children away,
providing hefty corporate usury
to scrub their little minds for the drive to the New Plantation...

We came back down, we came back down
from photosynthesis to the brick,
the woman's hospital
with its measured steps, its rectangular windows, its ruled basement

where they gassed us,
they gassed us, til we couldn't talk about Roosevelt or Eliot or Woodman or Truth
or Job or Tupac or Sanger. It's the Wild Wild West; no place
for wimmen, weak, disabled or dark;
guns riddled with laws in every clause.
We'd just settle in to what that means when,
later, you've copied your version of your own "Mind Kampf."

Nearly half our ladies could not strain to decide which way to go.
"Don't worry your little head about it, baby; we'll do the decision making
so you can do our most important work. Working makes you free!"

In sweet grim grasses, convection ovens, scattered
            underwear and scarves,   buckles   and candlesticks and scars,
               mothers and sisters and   old maids,
                        pens, words and faces drawn—
               scaredy boys hanging on to skirts or
                                    drooping stockings,
            looking up to our furrows of uncropped eyes—
                              we'd exchanged our muck and moss for blocks.

Led to undressing rooms where we were hung without bodies
      on hooks and herded, pregnant, into showers of elements precisely studied.
         They powered the world – their world,
                           our world,
               the worlds of everybody
                                 in the world -
                           taking the globe
            for granted, chop-shopping white marble monuments that broker no
silly googoos you'd only have to notice, feed and educate—
                     or stand their frilly moms or rights or rules--a city of men
               and only ME,

            ME, no tenement without rent, no single
                  occupant residency, no public pavilions for picnics or pondering aloud.

      It's a still life, sir, it's just a sketch; it's my country gasping. I begin to wonder--
      down to the camps with long aisles engraved with bloody knees, dorms set
                  like pews at Camp Witness, clouds of stench against clouds of rainbows—

will refugee women finally ghost out toward the trees
                  in heirloom veils, or will we start over in piles of gray, or will the photographs
                        of paintings fray and buzz across the projectors?
      This rough little squiggle shows somebody's
               chosen safety pins to mark this year's thriftstore throwouts;
                                 last year, somebody chose the stars.
                  What else will they choose? Who else
                        will be the chosen?

Miss Liberty, the Black Madonna

When she had so many years, hours, minutes to pray on both knees
in the groaning leaves grown in soft founts
           splashing from the long lashes of a *BLACK MADONNA*
        trickling from the Indus Valley to the dew in battlefields of the Old World,
             in a dribble along the heart of Egyptian gardens to
     splash across a Rhode Island rock
       onto a Maryland strawberry patch, glittering in dry rows down
              the plain green face of *LIBERTY*,
                  to Sand Creek, the Colorado, the LA River...

Her clients in bags out on the banks in a shed in a village in the dry stream bed of the Arroyo Seco,
    white eyes in a whited sepulchers,
           liquid red light streaming down
              drops...
                 Her back to the camera,
      kneeling, kneeling, shackles shattered,
           screaming down, "Breathe.

                     BREATHE!"

Flat on our backs, draped like a wounded marble full-grown baby in her lap,
    slapped,
        punched, massaged, begged, pleaded to
            Repent... Receive...!
            Repent... Receive! Wake up! Wake Up! WAKE UP, PLEASE!
            Repent, Repent, Receive, Receive. LIVE-LOVE, LIVE-LOVE,
            BREATHE! Oh, Live, now, Babies,
        listen to your Mama, now Breathe!

    Please... breathe... Please! breathe... now! breathe...Please! Please...
Please. Please... Please! PLEASE...

Sweat Lodge with a Healing Apache

Sometimes we notice.
       Then we think Someone is our enemy
              because he is very confused and tired.

    He has been fighting in many battles.
              He is battered from struggling.
          But he is not coming here as your enemy. The enemy
                    is outside of us.

If he came to you asking for your
       Blessing, he comes to you as a broken
         father and an unwilling warrior. He comes
            as a two-spirit or a four-spirit or an eight-spirit
       on his knees.

   It is not the pale skin, the white hat,
          that is a symptom, but the empty soul.

Sometimes they are using that sickness
              to divide us. But we recognize
    the same Water. We know there was a Beauty,
            hearing horses. We were all laughing
      together. We were smiling.

We do not have to be afraid, even
         of my sickness. The fire is here,
          inside this circle. It peers through the clouds.

     You can trust what the hummingbirds and the butterflies
  have been giggling to you.

Rain of the Feminine (Second)

They teach us the love of the very first rain,
the raining where the lightning is a yellow mist behind the blue mesas
far away, far-far-away in a swirl of rainbows
surrounded by billions of warm heavy
drops coming down
through flash and refraction in the twilight,
to kiss, to kiss, to kiss
our arms, our cheeks, the dirt, our uplifted lips
while we run and we run,
splashing and laughing the hope of
the rain.

A Letter to Fire

You are contained, like all of us, in both male and female, campfire and wildfire, stern punishment in bootcamp and spring training. You are not meant to kill, but meant to bless. I watched a trailer house burn to the ground. I have been thrilled in a campground of song and brainwash, encouraged to burn marshmallows and sticks of intention to loyalty to dubious cause, pledges of allegiance to suffering and sepulchers.

You have taught us with sage, with votive candles for the dead, prairie fire and LED headlamps on RAM trucks, the electric hum of the refrigerator that heals me as I dance.

When Raven brought the fire from the sun, he was a white bird, white as the white buffalo and White Shell Woman, and he had a beautiful song. But when he came in from the journey, he was suffering, his feathers scorched and ruffled and charred, his voice and become an ugly croak. We honor the raven for his sacrifice and do not laugh at his performances in the morning. But I wonder if he knew what he was doing? Would he have done this thing, gone so far as to bring the ember of that power back to us, if he had known what we would do with the energy, that we might be sustained to destroy the whole world?

The Egyptian pyramids of Giza, interpreted from the voices of native Egyptian scientists, have pointed the way to energy that is free, as demonstrated by Nikola Tesla. Water is free, managed and respected. Wind is free and healthy when honored. Land belongs to every person. Space is infinite, and can be experienced infinitely. Consciousness is free, a terrible power of beauty, truth and goodness. And fire is free, comforting, sustaining, in balance with both our needs and desires to do great things, build great cities and visit the galaxies.

When Jose Antonio Abreu set up a room filled with chairs and orchestral instruments and only eleven children showed up, when he raised his arms and pointed them to music, was he ever thinking he might be sustaining children of the poor, the marginalized, the disenfranchised of Venezuela? Could he have known he might show us the way to sustain our beggars on Grand Avenue? What a catastrophe that the world could be flooded with joy, when accountants could be working with piano makers. He lit a fire that warms the world with the music of Dudamel. Killing is suspended often in a choir.

I am writing to You, Fire, in gratitude for the lessons you have brought me.

SECTION TWO: Antelopes

Guardians

Well, I guess you can shoot
my herds of Antelopes, but not
the wise ones, not the funny ones,
the shy troop of guardians sent from
the deep of the storms in the north.

The elegant artistes are worse
than a cuffing by cops, with a tighter grip
and deliberation in the eye, like
they won't leave me, like
they love me; they make me -
reluctantly plump with wilderness
and goodness - to love them too,
to want to be near them,
to watch them back.

The Weaving

She thinks it hopeless.
Just has to sit down.
It's a lot to untangle and weave.
Woolly piles in burlap bags of smelly questions,
tangles of huff and puffs
after shearing, the washing, the eternity
it takes to dry.

Quit, surrender. Stay home,
safe inside her body again
no matter how far she had to go
to get there. Gotta like the quiet
in carding out the tangles;
it's gonna last forever.

Wooden paddles full of metal nails.
Untitled covers. Shakti.
Shakti, shakti, shakti, shanti,
shanti, shanti, shanti, shush,
shush. shush, shush, shush
Roll, comb and brush away
in a bag for the spinning and the dying,
the eternity it takes to dry.

When she sleeps she lays down
in a pattern grown in the ground beneath her,
eager one morning to rise to meet her
together to play on the loom
in a laughing room, storytelling and tapestry.

Wound Carving

No way to close or bridge that Canyon.
Only one way to get over it is to go through it.

You could take the turnoff around
in a wake of dirty haze,
Or copter over in a buzzzzzz if you're rich
in the myth of gilt magnificence... but

then you'd lose it, never knowing
in screwing it up
the glowing cold crackle of quiet in your light
time breathing in the blues...

Siren and a Scream

I came, from my own pain, to heal you; I wanted you...
that you not hurt anymore. I sat in our chair. "Would you like
a little bit more?" I'm asking.
I wanted to have a cup of coffee with you with your different face.
There is Indian Paintbrush in a glass vase.
Somebody laid a card on the Bible. The light of the lamp is subtle like petals of shadow.
The Pentateuch is so mean.
Your voice is soft and your shoes
make barely a tap, but the John you choose is the John of Revelations
and not The Beloved Disciple of love.
What is healing but a collaboration between the body and the medicine
and anybody who cares to visit? And if the medicine is wrong?
And if the body won't respond?
Do I read you poetry from your chair beside your bed,
and do you give me that look, that deep look that sees so little?
What good do words do,
what possible story could run around to dig back around to find the initial vision
and stamp it down?
It's already crippled the heart. These legs hardly walk.
I lean over in my chair, reaching out stroking your hair
to hear your murmur.
So sick, so spent, I can't be giving much.
But for a little while, before the ambulance gets here, I'll wait, you'll sigh.
We'll breathe together.
What is healing but a meeting of memory before the intensity
of little blue wheels on the walk
into the maw of the slamming of the doors,
between a siren and
a scream?

Abortion of a Woman

I find myself in an an acid creek,
the blister burn begins again
a blush in the skin
and then the smart, the flickering lap
of fire, paisley, swirl the blocks about my ankle bones
thighs, vagina, moans writhing up through the belly to the chin.

I drown down in, flickering, hissy
baby swaddled in copper barbwire
left on a stick in an irrigation ditch
birth canal tube of lava lips bubbling hissing,
see me, see me, see me.
I never asked to be divine, only cuddled. Kissed on the toes,
caressed, washed, perfumed, baby-powdered,
banqueted with my enemies and
sibling orphans in a crib in a kitchen
of bacon of toast of laughter,
hymns on the radio,
cotton denim and blue jersey,
flaming morning in the windows.
Is it just me, or was my mother
kidnapped to head start, heart stop,
seven generations from sanity,
kill the mother, save the monster?

The spirit lies wadded up in aluminum; no solution, no
resurrection or awakening now
to any balm or salve
beyond the stroke, the float in ocher lava, narrowing halls
in the roar of red gauzy rapids.

My Friend, My Illness

"Nobody's an enemy, really;
there're friends who will listen to you endlessly,
and teachers who go on and on."

        Friend, Friend, Friend,
        Friend, the cook, my encephalopathy,
        the invalid in the room—

      Friend, Friend, Friend,
      Friend, the mocker in the dark
      with a shattered glass
      of spilling Moon—

    Friend, Friend, Friend,
    disgruntled uncles for organs
    too drunk to work
    but still kind, benign.

  Friend, Friend, Friend,
  Friend of the Bird in the broken window,
  that beautiful bright Smile
  that left me for a month on a world cruise—

Friend, Friend, Friend,
Friend, the Moon that left me a loon
with Presence in wood wind rhythms
in a global arrangement in jazz.

<u>*Nesting Doll*</u>

This woolly cocoon, this hospital blanket,
the doll in the doll in the doll in the doll
in the distant myths late twilight storytelling time,
staring coldly through the X-Ray into the shell of the bone,
the abandoned baby screaming, screaming, screaming
for touch.

Ah, there was another history somewhere,
where she drifted whispering like evening snow
or an awful gray dream squall across the gray of the cold Atlantic.
Heavy with baggage and hope
in romantic nationalism, a longboat sliver on a rope,
could we be free?

Can we ever be free? The gray ships
float heavy through the red cell sea in the coagulate of sunset, chugging,
chugging, chugging out of the Nordic light
to night and more mountains. You are mine,
mine, mine (I made you; you make me) doll
in the doll in the doll in the doll mama, my bones
screaming through the mouth of the infected wound.

Antelope in the Canyon

I found grasses of bliss, succulents of journeys,
savory manna,
honey and wheat cream.
Hunted the holy grail,
companionship, adventure and dance.
In the beginning was always the work of the word, the meadowlark,
that tiny yellow bird on a stick in the morning.
My bliss was the pinon nut fresh from campfire.
My bliss was the guitar and the harmonica and the flute and drum.
Where do I find it again?
My back is against the cold wet rock of the dark.
Outside they hunt me like a Jane doe, hundreds hunting,
flannel shirts and metal creeping,
in creaks, the rocks,
the shade, the glades, the only spring.
I come to the last hole. And hide.
The sand is a wash under my hooves.
I am alone.
I have discovered Antelope Canyon,
rays raining beauty through white
space on the shoulders,
thighs of gold, my fingers slide
along the cool sweat of sandstone
and I am in heaven.
Hunted.

Treatment Resistance

There's reasons you led her to water
                        and can't make her drink:
          She's got her own bucket,
          too sick to lick,
          or your own bucket's full of lye.

Sometimes you need
          to check the barn,
          call a doc,
          or sniff your own bucket.

Never seen a healthy thirsty mare
          won't roll and splash and play
          in a flowing river of pure clean water
          on a hot summer day.

Respond

Want to feel alive? Feel dead first.
Feel the dank fog pause down Long Beach Boulevard,
windshield and bumper souped in a smog
stop suffocate bucket seat cell when radio sell says somebody's out There
but they'll never hear you, wifi not invented, and you did it on your own
then...

be rescued.

Feel you've died, cuddled with an old pink bear
Shuddering, window riddled with shot,
rattling floor coughed up your selves
a rockfall grandslam mudslide avalanche in dark tight tidied shelves,
maps and mysteries, books for Calculus and the Honshu tea set
then...

be rescued.

Want to be alive?
Dive slide again down in the empty riptide
surge of sea muscle lust of disinterested force
out to pop shock of oranges on a plane, red dye run set between gasp and choke
then...

be rescued. Then...

hot arms with black hands like honey hams
white sheets to lay down in,
wrapped, crisp and clean guttural touch, a sip, a sob in a dream
then...

feel rescued. Then notice
you have been rescued. Be curious about it.
Then
respond...
Respond... Respond... Respond.... Respond... Respond

...

I Loved You, Finally

I was a broke pony, untamed,
eyes wide and whitened with terror (I'd seen everything), I thought,
I was dancing in the grass today, in the kitchen,
in the moon, sun streaming in the window,
and your song came on...
Your song of the primary color in your fingers, rose gold, copper, sad blue God
and Payne's gray, the sable of the brush, your tongue on my skin,
the white canvas, marble as the Taj Mahal,
and after all the years, the years, the years
of waiting for the wound to close, it opened from mi corazon, gushing,
bright red, good blood, and lively out over the memory,
my bare ankles on the floor, my knees,
and to you who loved me eagerly with your eyes, your brush,
and I finally loved you in a sudden rush.
Thank you for the joyous sin, the Kahlo garden,
the anguish, the weakness, by which I remember you, top of the temple in Yucatan,
bottom of the alley
between the Thirteens and Diamonds through the brown glass
in the lamp, the mission, its huge wheels imagining
trudge, thud, the ranks of the "saved" in brown chains of children and daisies
thudding, thudding, swallows return, the blue sky of sand, your laugh,
your hunted eyes, portrait of the Mayan,
heads rolling to appease the energy of fire, loving
brokenly, ran me white mane, flame-carved in titanium design.
I remembered
your bones, your breath, your salty warmth,
and finally, this dance with your presence a minute
dawning this permission to love you.
You loved me as only a painter of sunsets loves clouds.

Apple Dumplings for Tesla

Nikola Telsa was a mentally ill immigrant who fell in love with a pigeon and discovered the electrical system for Alternating Current. Which is why light bulbs work. Tesla was working on a communication system for ships at sea. He believed energy is everywhere, and free ... when the pigeon died. What if some poor old lady had invited Tesla in for apple dumplings, a cup of lemon grass tea and some poetry? Would there be so many awful telephone poles? Would there be more deep green forests of pine trees?

It's like: Shh, sh, sh, sh, shhhh.....! Kindness is here now... Energy is everywhere and free.
   Mommy... Mommy?   Mommy??! ...Mama!! Mamaaaa!
   Mama?... Mother. Oh...   Mother. Oh, Mom.... Oh.... God...

     Kindness is here now. Sh, sh, sh, sh, sh....
    Energy is everywhere, and free... shhhhhhhh...
 Mommy is murmuring through him
    a whizz with the electricity of honey,
  the brain yokey and running on, needing stirring,
       needing kneading left and right,
    needing a little squeeze, and a poke
 in the pineal gland and in the beautiful ugly amygdala
      and in the heart and the bones
        and everything down in there...
    to the right big toe and the wet wool
   sock on the sole...
      ...and, the shock of spilled milk.
    She is more than
  measurements of watts and tables of charges;
We are the vibrato in her fingers and in her blouse.
    Simply, held - she holds...
       She loves when she is cuddled.
     Sh, sh, sh, sh, sh! Kindness is here now.
   Energy is everywhere, and free.
SHHHHHHHHHHHHhhhhhhhhhhhhhhhhhhhhhhhhhhhhhhhhhhhhhhhhhhhhh.............

Chocolate Banana Cream Mother

I am my mother.
She comes home
in the rain to bake
a chocolate banana cream pie.

She is sitting in the living room
when I come in, to scooch the blanket up around my ears. Sometimes she's smiling.
She holds me, cooing, simpering,
holding me up to sniff,
changing me day after day; she has
that much love from the father.
"Oh, let me look at you, you beautiful thing!" she murmurs,
observing my little digits. Sometimes she spanks.
She withholds the brownie
until after the dishes are done, even the pans.
After eight o'clock, its time to be taxed with the father,
for the contagion
or the PTA, or the Obee Gine
or my oopsy daisy. I regard me.

She makes me do my business plan…
Because I can either do it or I can't,
she refuses to pay my flight to Philadelphia.
She finds the time
because she loves her life and her home;
she goes to the City of Love to advocate
because she so loves
me, my brother and the father.

Johnny Appleseed Pie

You got the lace across the table and they are really trying
not to bang pitchforks on the table.
You are master, Chef. Do not serve them roots for fruit.
They've grown through the winter.
Bring them apples out on Wedgewood,
wiped along the edge,
pastry so fine you listen,
thin on thin shell sunlight
tincture of lemon
exquisite crunch of warm
white cream in clean chiffon custard.
They've waited so long surviving; do not toss them dirty root in a bark,
but thought-out sharp apples in fresh egg
yolk whipped and heated, laughed up
in a comforter of cracked wheat,
sweet almonds, honey of sage, roasted
in a bare blush of salt of
Himalayas.

Don't shovel them the labor or strain,
cuisine them the moment
the fork of juice drop
drips along the lip
that they might live in joy forever. They'll be back
for more. They'll do anything
for it. They'll love you like
you love your crusty pie and baking.

Rain of the Feminine (Third)

They teach us the dance of female rain. They teach us a living
in oscillating silver, of jumping the sagebrush
or flying past the feathers in the cedar trees,
panting, joking and surging down profound gullies to hold back
with our chests and our fingers the flow, the rivers of mud,
at the last minute to be plummeted out of the way
by a brown benediction
pouring through
like a frisky truckers' caravan
down Rabbit Ears Pass.

Letter to Earth

Stone, Rock, Crystal, Clay and Titanium, You have loved me. When I was weak and terrified, the children unrelenting in bullying, touching my child to arouse me, You wrapped me in plaster. My back became strong, and my soul found strength for the next hard thing that I would have to lift. You gave me the sandstone boulders on El Huerfano to climb before I knew her first name. Her first name was something like, "The Mountain Surrounded by This People." She was the place of rattlers and holy water.

Structure, routine, you gave me an elementary school. The blue and gold leather basketball I got for my birthday taught me boundaries on an enclosed court with a team. I got a pair of red converse tennis shoes with rubber soles. My mother provided me the canary yellow in the living room we shared with so many people. She taught me to make animals and villages of salt and flour playdough. My father taught me exploration with no maps but with the eye and the pickup and the boots, and he taught me how to carve wood.

My guitar was strung with steel strings that moved as I touched them. They sang gently back to me in waves and frequencies. My piano had black and white keys so that I could easily find the violet to yellow harmonies in the rainbow of the Goddess. Chemicals and minerals, brushes of wood and fur, pens of plastic filled with ink that I could smell and touch and see. You grounded me by bringing these goods to my senses.

Then you gave me outlines, and the reams of rectangular paper, lines and grids, rules and laws, music theory and literary criticism in finite books. From scream to cry to mama to music to poetry. We have five fingers. Five senses. These are curious, revealing the negative space between them.

You provided finity. You provided rhythm in the mathematics of music, a tabernacle hub from which to move toward freedom in community. We work in materials, from the imagination flowing like water over rocks, cement, sand, freefall and swimming pools. You provide ceramics to serve the universe in banquet halls and tipis. Gandhi said, "How do you eat an elephant?" Well, never mind. You have taught me how to feed the fussy baby, to swaddle him gently and to let him run with feet across the earth, to fly when he is ready. One drop of rainbow honey in a spoon at a time.

SECTION THREE: Bear

Kermode Bear

Sometimes I got this fat pale
black bear going through the pails,
claw fishing lox, coffee grounds
and gooseberries
with that familiar ungainly dance
of hairy ballet, tolerated,

bragged about later
in student research or a video.
I'd take care not to catch her alone
in Hiber Nation, starving
and defensive, heavy happy,
and grumpy growly with cub.

In Search of Excellence

In a perfect world, there would be
alabaster cities, whited monuments,
no mountains. Our stormy seas would be
pragmatically filled in.

Our climate would be seventy two degrees
with a gentle breeze. There would be no art
and no science, no villages weaving
psychedelic baskets, no doctors or nurses, no
frightened mothers or kids, janitors or actors
or other dirty workers. Because, in a perfect
world, everybody would be white, in
business, six foot six, and physically fit.

In a perfect world, we would all be men,
some discernable white would be the shade
of our skin, and we would all be descended of
New England, attorney, businessman,
empiricist and rational, exclusive of all sense
but what is on the surface now in front of our
eyes, sparing the expense for the elegance
of covers on the lenses.

There would be no pre-existing condition
or noncompliant wimmin, just white men
in business, STEM or education, six foot six
and physically fit, with the courage
to stand up and be number one,
not number two and not three billion, with
I.Q.s of not less than one hundred and seven.
We'd all get along then, like mossy bones.

Our communication would be so deep;
no Mandan, Italian, Cheyenne, Swahili or
Chinese. Or readjustment. Or interest.

There would be no hummer drivers, humor,
SWAT or foreign mercenaries, happily using
last year's incendiaries, there would be no
independent nations. No need for chics,
checks or law: Strong, educated businessmen
by intuition, know it, buy it. We would all be
Jobs.

A perfect world would have no birds, not
being human, except some scraggly eagles in
executive branches. Everything else would be
legally drugged, rotted in a breathing bed.
Dead.

In a perfect world, there would be no moon,
no night, no silence, no softness, no violet,
no curves — curses, but no protesters or
news, because, think, there'd be a lot of
omniscient men just doing good business,
lights-out manufacturing without the
technicians, and these white guys would be
rich, and lonely.

We would all be fair, clean, handsome,
six foot six, and physically fit, and, oh,
I am sorry, sorry, in a perfect world,
love love love love love your Self, 'cuz
there would be no male heirs or rheumy gaze.

Fear Itself

My fear is not a man, he's
not an animal, it's
not a wicked witch, she's
not alien robots on fourteen appendages, they're
not a chemical attack;
fear is a feeling,
fear is a thing.

When the thing that is Fear comes
skulking to the door, when
I don't recognize the character,
can't place the gloom of the space,
can't remember what the thing that
fear does does.

Does he burn, does it bite,
does she hex, do they fight,
am I oozed down screaming
in the acid? What do I do?

There are two things to fear,
the fear and the Thing.
There are lobes and glands and skin and anatomy parts
squeamish to burn, be bitten, be cursed and beaten,
a repealing off these pink lips in the blackening.

I can handle the fear
every day; I just haven't the feeling
what to do with
the Thing.

Blancabear

I am barely human, but I am alive,
                come down from North
          hot wind and wildfire, to scrounge in the bins for a can
of green tamales and a scrap of leftover sole.

        Have you seen my Grandma? They say before
she was Blackfoot she was a black Madonna,
               beaten so hard she left us
      to the rich man who gagged her and choked my mommy;
he liked to work us, he loved the circus;
        he liked to eat meat.

     I'd like to meet my mama now they say
          she's being fed, owns her own alley. I was down,
in the valley, when I saw her gray shadow once in a dream.
            She looked like a queen!

But, hey, you with the flashlight, guess you must have heard me
        banging around back-clacking on the tincan bins?
Ain't too late I'm begging you, let us lie down awhile
       in your national park. Pilgrims, tourists or investors
         will never even notice
the lumps in the drifts of the snow.

      Come Spring we'll head back North
to see what they done to my cousins
         in the woods, and my sisters and their kids
     on the ice flow. Who knows,
maybe we'll find them starting to recover,
        snow dancing with the aurium of the falls.

The Götterdämmerung

"Art is not the performance,
but the altered state in behavior of participants at the exit."

He heard the beautiful harmonies in the frequencies and loved the staffs,
the clefs. He wrote the notes as they were dictated.
Dozens of them. Thousands of them, notes for flutes and notes for violins
and the notes the most dramatic music.

Then he went to Paris where he was disrespected by the Jews. He was penniless and sour,
hungry, mean, unforgiving, blame the many for the few, and his rage increased.

They told him he'd never make it in music; they disrespected him.
So he went back to Germany and did an opera,
fifteen hours of the Ring Cycle.
The political thugs he pleased were inspired
to build a thousand camps to end in revenge
anyone with difference.
What can be done with the notes on a page

and the grudge of a chip of embers on the shoulder,
when humans are contagiously inspired to hate together?
The corpses pile up on hidden film, the idols
stinking ashes in pages of rages.

But what if, whatever is finished is love, the icon,
the endangered soloist, knowing the goodness,
audience in performance
in this company, kneeling,
spent, together in the whirling clouds of the witness in the movements
of galleries of galaxies?

<u>American Gypsy in a German Barn</u>

I found my dirty falling down barn on your farm,
cool corner of the warm shade,
lunch of sardines, two cans, three rolls of
pumpernickel and a laugh and a bottle
of Watermelon Mineral Spring Water, on my way
out westway, refugee of London.

If I could find a safe space of stone
with a flue for the night, we could be fine. A safe
space free of chemicals and shuffling boots,
dry hay and empty wind.
But you didn't want me, coming out, scared, in a rage.
You said that old homestead belonged to you.
You built that fireplace. And I can only see
the shovel, the boots, the yellow teeth
fire in the ticking anymore
in the middle of a manger of terror.

But I had nowhere to go but the manger I'm found.
You the gray administrators cannot be tending
wildfire by pretending it is contained in a benign
grim. And in the aftermath, you might wonder
whose cow it was, or whose weary milkman,
you are the owner, you locked us all in together,
in a bunker, one nation united,
ignited in a bully market,
and I am telling you now, we're burning down... Fire! Fire!

Here's a crack hole, here, down in the bullcrap,
just take the knee with me.
Then head for the woods still standing.

War Dance

(The Day Before We Beat Custer)

Jagged obsidian night.
Encamped along the twilight of the purple creek.
Somebody's coming, in cowboy hats.
We sit by the slow fire, little bodies flickering in and out between us all.
The people have to think.
The strangers are hundreds and hundreds of miles away from law.
The headman is looking down.
The old women brood.
The skins of our fortresses flap in the wind.
They are coming with tanks and tear gas,
armed with stare decisis to shred our homes;
they want to burn the rivers;
they want to eat the hills.

"I am here. You go do this, you go do this."
"You take your warriors and run around behind."
"You keep the campfires burning."
"You go this way."

Jail is the home of our youth.
Our families are slaves to pride.
The Mandans have all died.
Everyone is crazy.
The medicine people forgot who they are chanting for.
Our mothers and grandmothers have no time to care in the chaos.

"You wait for this one." "You send a message."
"You watch; all of you guys, watch."

We are losing the land.

Wear your animals, your protectors.
Let the smoke of sage waft all around you.
Cleanse your medicine pouches.
Bless your children. Look at your cousins.
Hold hands. Paint the shield. Gather the bows.
Dance without fire.
Custer is coming.

"You do the sweat." "You take them to the valley." "You hide."
"You run." "You smile and walk." "You pray."
"You dream." "You dance." "You fight."

We may have many battles to fight after we win the battle in the morning.
The sun will give us the signal.

"You go that way." "You talk to the Chamber." "You go over there." "You take the day off."

"You have a cup of coffee with five good friends."
"You gather the children to go."
"You close the store."
"You pick up the people at the convalescent home"
"You take pictures."
"You have a feast at your house."

It will seem that we are here. We will not be here,
but we will be here. We are going to march to vote.
He is coming again. We will be here,
ready for them.
Wish we could've voted
for either independence or democracy the first time.

Mandated Reporters

"Eggs in a carton do not have the destiny of eggs in a nest."

Pressured down through your aluminum hall to pay the mortgage,
while your clients do not have a home,
debtor to the university that trained you to be so
cold, refined, dead and vague,

you know what they do
to our elders in restraints who laugh in there.
Were you ever Enough that you didn't have to push it?
Did you ever have a friend more than a colleague?
Did you know your mother?
Can you think about it?
Can you start over?
Were you ever oppressed,
Filipino, Irish, Ghanaian, Armenian, Jew, Chinese?
Did you ever aspire to be a professional nurse,
from a lost tribe or people or country?
Did you ever seek competence in divine humanity?

You know what they do
to the orphans and the shamans in there.

Didn't you garden in the dream
you traded in for a long hall with no wind, no sun, a bleached
pimply pimp of a parody cop?

And you know they're paid,
leering at the teenage boys and girls in there.

Wasn't the world ever, ever enough,
its water, its woods, its bricks of clay, it's cotton fluff, its tumbling blue effervescence
you've leveraged for kindness, its balance, its wild,
for cash, control and counterfeit chrome?

When you know what forty thousand nurses
are doing to the disabled in there.

You have your reputation with the abusive Director
                                        you only know by his acronym,
                    author bio, or the pretty calligraphy on the plate rim
of salmon and arugula at the Conference at the Hilton.
                    You pay for your Mercedes with your soul and your "clients"
                         insurance, road-raging freeways
when you could be camping, but you're driven by trauma, your mama,
                    to compounds of confinement in windowless cells,
                              paper talking, anonymous stalking and petty notes?
          They are your peers.
     What have they done to you, then,
                         that you bought it, stayed on? How much
                              homeowners, car and health insurance debt
          does it take to make the slave the bully?

You stay out of it, but you know what the doctors are doing
to the future of the loners in there.

Call Del Amo or Huntington, Della Martin, Methodist,
                         County, Verdugo, Ingleside or I don't care.

You know what the "guards" doing
to the blacks and the browns
with no PPOs in there.

Whatever happened to teamwork, Coach?
Whatever happened to Thomas Jefferson?
Whatever happened to sanity, Doc?
What ever happened to humanity, community?
Whatever happened to nursing?
Whatever happened to hatching?

Social Work USA

"Mental illness" was a headache,
                        a car accident, a missing mother,
         a weird flutter of the eye, a genetic diagnosis,

before he got swept to the edge, flung headlong into the jagged bubbles,
     homeless, cold, running without your phone for 911,
                     without your webs and your meds,
       blood-streaked spray of an emergency
  from which you pretend to drag him,
          chained, crazy, freaking, by now
                buddy-buddy with the stones and the frozen dead.

You could have let him keep his home,
     at first bewildered along the easy river,
       fifty miles up,
         could have modeled courage, swam with him to the bank,
            but you couldn't decide: expense, risk, scrap?

     You chose to have him go on over and now they've got him,
  the currents of bleach and serrated rocks,
      and they've got you, too, your proud degrees,
your red-painted skiff,
     your threads, your shell of kindling,
   your department watching with looks of horror at the twenty-thousand
          peer-reviewed books of statistics at your disposal
   from the safety of the banks.

     You'll want to do something. More is coming.
   You may have to move from your comfortable
    house you bought on the banks down by the river
       to appreciate its giggling by in awesome blues.

Hollow Word World

Inuit to German scientist, 1930's.

"Hey, what you doing up there dancing around the Poles?"
Huh, why, looking for bubbly fresh-water seas inside,
hunting for underwater tunnel to the underside in
the manic swing of some compass in the iris, the porch the door to
the underworld in the hole of a round spool. What'd you think?
Might be where to emigrate sometime,
my soul, the north pole, the word hollow center of the churning world.
Grass might be bluer there and greener here, but
the Hollow could be Paradise, lukewarm, not burning down,
no fossil fuel or telephone poles, titanium to rape for, uranium
to mine by slave, traffic and interchange, huh, what's the chance of that?,
(hadn't invented bitcoin and cards to keep
the nomads off the bus or swept the wilderness camps with howitzers or dozers,
hadn't burned the terrarium to the shell of the surface, so what's the chance of that?)
Ah, you know, no se, Columbus and Standish immigrated to heaven, ingested
with the Monster that divested the vestiges of every leaf of grass and crook
of a creek in the meadow in the valley, Old Spain New Spain,
New England Nicetown in the city of brotherly love, indivisible with liberty and justice and all.
Can't take this-land-your-land, might make this-land-my-land laid out
free on the surface of the globe,
like a helpless, fevered cling of endometrium to momma,
a still point of the kerning world defined in
New Iron Mountain, New Chicago Dump in Antelope Valley.
Huh, I may discover the book to be a giant cave of a sleeping lady,
the unfriended dragon, the Iroquois,
or shady spring shared, a Pueblo kiln or healthy baby, or a shelter of the overhanging rock.
But, oh, my Love, let glory alleluia gurgle in the gastric; I can't stay home, forget the hope
in the dark whale Eye in the ice flow, the plop plop fizz fizz tummy turn to
Heil. Hell. Heel. Hail. Or Heal, and Hallelujah.

I'm Using My Voice

Why'd they jump?
Why is the GNP sinking
and the mortality rate so high?
Why do people die?
And why do I get to live sick in the sandstone, turquoise dawn,
the porcupines, cottontails and coyotes,
lightning and feminine rain,
newspapers, colored comics, the books of Whitman and Karo Ska
side by side peach yogurt, free in the library at the university
with the spoken-word chant of John Trudell,
the fellowship of slavery to Spoken Word?

What good did a gun ever do?
We can't remember the grandfathers;
and we can't remember to pick up the children.

I'm telling a story to myself. An adventure.
I tell it to you.
I dedicate my body, this temple, these old adobe ruins in the canyon.
I'm using my life to ask one question,
And I'm using my voice
For the answer.
Maybe I'll come up with it by the day I die...
The question I ask is
Why?

How Walls Are Moved in the Canyon

Minerals find their sparkling
      cleaning the hauls, scrubbing eternal bearing
walls that deliver deep layers of sulfur, the gold
     we suffer, the cracks of black and blues bleeding
in the bones, white crusts under tables
      articulating gravity drip by
           drip
      by drip by
        drip by drip
     by drip to
      drop
trickling down leathered seems in babbling
   scenes in quicksand
      years below,
         wandering through hunched crystal
    fossils and sentiment etched and moved by
     cold crystalline rising to
  the drying thirst
in the living.

Rain of the Feminine (Fourth)

The lightning colliding in the distance
        and the old desert drowning in bliss
                        and the neckbones connected to the headbone
            and the crows all staring in a caw,

your grade-point average all forgotten,
        and the dress will be forgiven by your mother-in-law
                    car bills are all stacked and buried under
            and you are finally going to graduate!

the perty perky neighbor girl is winking right by
        and the revolution's set back a little later
                        the tomato bugs all in a stupor
            and the plane is going to wait til we get there,

        And that garden of Mary Contrary is going to blister,
    going to burst, going to born you a bumper crop!
            They teach us to dance in spring raining.

Letter to Open Spaces

Surely you surround, being inside of me, inside of my heart, my gut, my bones, my reservoirs of water. I need only dance to discover you again. If I close my eyes you are in the museum of my walls reflected there. If I unblink, if I lift one shutter, I can know you.

In Hong Kong cages, in a medical "clinic" with bullet-proof glass, where there are no windows, in a room of restraint or in a great rotunda of music or power, and even in a cast of plaster, there is abundant space, connected through tunnels and mind to infinite light. I am.

I fidget a pinky in the light of the morning. You.

In us, in silence, in the rests, the halls of Dudamel and Brahms, in the backgrounds and eyes of an online Anansi Workshop, we find space. In the Super Bowl and the constriction of a psychiatric office, there is infinite Room, infinite understanding. After every haiku is a line of silence. After every line of poetry, there is a rest. The music is in the open spaces.

In the warmth of my mouth where I sometimes swaddle my tongue like an a fussy foster baby, there is freedom. When I bite it like Michael Jordan hanging back a moment to see, and then to be, be held, before the slam, I feel the space, the Spirit in my mouth, from the toes up through the crooked paths to find the next basket of gift. Oh, give me liberty. Or give me death. Give me certainty. Or give me choice. Let me still my tongue forever in Your audience.

Open Space: it is the flight of prayer and meditation, the simplicity of a petal and the desert after the Red Sea. You are the Bodi tree and hours hung suffering from the sky in effigy, the Zen garden, the tangle of mud tunnels the divers must navigate to find the lost team of celebrating players. You are bonsai. You are the bridge of a tanker facing the jagged peaks in crossing the great water.

You create in the aftermath of broken rocks the echo. Echoes. Nam Myojo Renge Kyo. The Lotus Moon. The Dawn and Requiem. The hymn. There is no sin. There is only yahateh and muy bueno, if you only understood. Your god is Gud. Love is God. Come forth, no need be sick in a sepulcher. You are the mind of architecture. You are the rocket that presses with fire against the ground, using empiricism for full effect. You are the woman and children and the man in the house, their laughter. You are always mine. Free as long as I am.

SECTION FOUR: Coyote

Shapeshifting

Sometimes I am Coyote,
trotting past to trick me into
seeing things, as they are, seeing me,
the blue guitar. Laughing
it out loud later.

The Day Before I Loved

I'd come to beg for everything except my life. On the day before recovery, a dizziness of a whiz,
a metal mosquito, buzzed my ear. "It's over. Baby, it is so over."
Somebody said to me (on the day before I lived)
you can make the summit of Mt. McKinley,
shear freeze, deep blank mukluks
like paper, if you want to repair you,
if you take it at a step or two.
Yeah? It's at least a full day later, I'm a granite mute encased in ice,
knarled toes blue now, needing
ropes, a stiff back, the clank of belay device
and axe, the need of my companion...
But I see now the bubbling, the clouds in the orchard valleys of another country.
more than one height, capped by a bad bald grin, Prussian blues
and jagged. I see the point,
a shaky step along cut-glass.
My climber inner mama finally sighs, "You gotta come on down now," refocusing round
to slodge back down all those pitches, that frost,
those rocks (cracks
like sharks lurking behind the slideshow).
I have to twist aside another second. Was it real?
What am I, waiting for forever a moment in thin air, having met
the Day Before who, with a half-glass of blush, almost glibly introduced me to her Day After.
The two of them are so very, very close. Thirty years
apart, they both look better together than alone.
A bunch of us are camping, same ground,
basecamp,
tomorrow,
just saying, wanna join us.

Spider Woman Haiku Pine Boxes

"If they give you lined paper, write the other way." —WC Williams

an old pond frog jumps in sound of water	blank line for worship silence is nothing sans trembling dew	E equals MC Square
Basho algorithm cool	One moment?	German/Jew tired on a bike

Center leaping Splash and cash in the photo flash	Toad cold in a glass dish jerks with poke	Evidence Base FillintheBox Compliance
"Daaaaddd?! Who in the world is Michael Jordan?"	Nonwaka waka	Norwalk Metro Cemetery Who were they? No box

---

Waves. Bites. Clinical epitaphs in plots Check in the kitchen	No treble in the web No frog. No fly. No flash of do	Spider Rock top Bone flour children whip-schooled white.
Research labs for MediCaid No sight in sight but oversight	Nagasaki Temple No rest. No peace.	Tseyi Canyon Professional tourists

---

For Devin Laing, Stewart Lupton, LADMH, Jasmyn Ha Eng, Heather Wilcox

Bears in the Bloody Snow

Furry smelly bear fury
hard by a frozen screen of the tech talk pond
heavy skinny pawing on pane of ice, a black claw wicked for digging
as a sloth's claw, in trail of little badger, bunny track, chickadee small-print clause
curve and polish bearing dirty down deep a rectangular window
bloody with moon in a mourning pool, tapping time in the crimson snow
disturbed back offgrid to the grizzly woods before...,
before fires of crowds before
canned spaghetti turnoffs
with stoplights banging tin lids,
when you could hibernate...
before fords, haunts, nongoose honk,
bibles,
national parks,
calls and
snow hats, mittens...
before masks,
when you could still bear touch
and sniff and bare and roll around and play in the honey in the bushes
before scrounging frozen fish sticks, bugs and plastic berries... ...scratch,
scratch, scratch, scratch,
whiteout...

scratch, scratch, scratch, scratch, scratch, comb and brush, tap, TAP, CCRRRAAACK,
SPLASH! HEY!
See, zoom, ZOOM! That's us! rainbow reflections
radiating our scruffy old ears in cold cold
copper diamond dawn! Oh, baby, hurry!
UNMUTE!

Bees Don't Belong in No Class

Fuzzy chubby buzzy refugee of colony collapse
disorder got caught in the windows, buzzing through the screen,
and they're all looking up at her like,
"Hey, honey bees don't belong in no class!"
And it's a stir, and it's a scream,
I'd ask, show her out the screen
through the window
or open a door, but she's frantic, she's a little frightened,
confused, lonely, banged up, hive closed down
with just a queen and a bunch of nurses,
hovering over the kids in their little box beds
and all the worker bees gone or dead
Caught in a worm hole she thought was a warm hall,
she fluttered in, shuddering and vibrating
in the idea pretty fast that
bees with stripes don't belong in no class
with the professor and the truant officer,
the man from admin, fifteen grad students
and the janitor with a broom and a net and a stick and a pen
fifteen books and a library next door;
All she can hear is the swishy swish swish,
and the shouts and screams
the buzz of the flutter of her fat wack wings
of that genetic stinger on that big yeller hairy ass;
Bees just might not belong in no class, but
she got nowhere to run,
no home, no fly, only the worm hole she found in the screen
through a crack in the glass, and it might be crass but maybe
bees don't belong in no class.

But you know, more than the warm
and the storm outside, what really got her was
the jazz,
a hope
of the band and the study of the notes.
She's crazy drunk with the wifi.
The rhythms soothe her,
so she doesn't really care anymore
if she gets smashed for a taste
of the swoon, the storytelling of mothering
suffering, the old warriors drumming out proud
again as it was in the rooms of gold in the past,
the dance in the honeycombs
now nothing but catacombs,
She thought she saw the million-faceted
eyes of her mother there
in the soft hands on the pages,
the songs from the books, the sob of the glory, the stop signs, the streets,
the comfort of the grammar, the ellipses and the dash,
and, God, if she sits on the wall in the corner
will they let one lost bee in from the burning ash? To let
this little bee belong just a little in the class?

The Revolutionaries

(Friend, or More. But Not Less)

I see you hiding in windows, hiding with a 'cocktail' behind
a water barrel in the wild, wild west, a beautiful wolf
from another guerilla company and I want you.

In another game, you might be Sami, and I warn you
or you New English or German, South African or
Indian Resistance, sexy with petroglyphs
down your shoulders and across the belly, honey,

Down, Down! Incoming!!! Will you be mine?
What is it about Stout and Tequila, Sauerkraut and sheep gut roasted on a stick, Falafel and
yogurt from Ulan Bator? The BBQ? Money is the monster,
enemy of me and mine, he comes on with a grin
and a Coke meme,
he hardens, comes on, comes on, touching the senses
marketing his need into the bullets we make
ourselves, non fungible tokens in bars we choose
to pay virtual reality fake-like sitting meditation,
in the student union, backwards, stillborn; instead
of Be Coming from love, we are torn
untouched selves desiring no beauty but porn,
plasticized one-sense store counterfeit for Soul/
Power/
Communion/
Spirit/
Flow/
Present/Finale of Creation.

Sun Kissed

"Unless a man be born again,
he will not see the kingdom of God."

If I gave you a piece of my mind today,
it wouldn't be a Petrie dish of gray,
blood splat of oil and fat.
It would be orange today,
a mix
of red and yellow,

halfway to the bloody crush
of stone queries set in eyes at dusk;

halfway to the shining of chandeliers
in trillion champagne quartz, waltz
of lemon lace along the wall
of the short of the long inaugural ball.

My thinking this morning
is bumpy and sweet with a little sour
and a shot of vitamin C
inside its thick skin.
But nobody talks about that. Your finished product is
a legal yellow document
with a billing code
coded, read
in Arial RED.

Thin Blue Line [Sky I]

"It is not a ballet; it is a wreck in a rocket
in a cloud like winter, lost map and no sexton, no pilots,
having to trust the pirates."

Believe in Sky, it's all the why we do
               in the long dark hauls
        where smell and touch is the only thing,
                     where we learn what characters mean.
            In the flap of wet, rent-free burlap, here,
      hear the complementary acoustics you breathe in cathedrals
                       and caves of vacant echo, a scream Hello!?"
          the broadcast of your first cut
                     solo, choraled and rapt
             and sung in the sol of a son
        playing in a corner, alive for now.
         No twitter and beer, just humans in skins
  having lost our minds to the joke
     to study the hope
         to get back on track later, steady...
                Later, right?, back to the gate of the tarmac
     on to the seat of the pants!
         Remember Sky,
                  he's in the rolling,
    that blanket of love that swaddles you...

Mayim, Mayim (Thirst)

From a Dance Meditation, "See, Hear, Love"[9]

"I am thirsty again, having tasted water."

Morning. Light. Fog,
            I am raven
yesterday. There are other birds. Hummers, flutterers, funny birds, roadrunners,
                          raptors. I respond to the beat
of a world, sometimes solo. Sometimes duet. Sometimes
        choir. Fire. Maybe this is how being
                  alone together brings us back over and over to being
          together,
         alone. Nonperformance. Conscious   unconscious.

Lamentation in the Depression
           on the day I was again borne of dance water, I said no:
     Cells locked up; clammed
    shut. The wind laughs spasms among fingerbone blue
            tow and tug of
        rolling-chasm-echo wave wall re-verb swingsong sung in puzzle bone
beads strung along sockets and springs of scrolling yellow myths of a sketchy
          old skull
        speaking.
     Livingcolor mono-moment met, once we moved
   through
arroyo-seco flat stone-sea marble tomb-shone cockleshells like
             red vines of hard-sand sunseed set. Lifted, still,
     curved, carved, orange-cloud starlight. Stop. Beginning
        again.

---

9   www.medicinedance.com

A Company of Friends

To an ER doctor

Your world will not end
if you stop struggling, to rest.
It might if you don't.
Seek the people in the crowd
who are your friends.

You will know them
because they will remember
your name.
They will laugh at your jokes.
They will touch you.
They will see you.
They will offer you things.
They will always come back after a fight.
That trip you've been on ends
on the other side
of the planet, right here.

You can stop now.
People will be kind to you
because you have found them.
You can march your body
right out of the tank of an army
to feel, in a field of the players
of lasting change.

Dolphins in Pods

"A programmer cannot teach a buffalo how to swim to Nairobi"

Time is not the private
property of me, I am not free
but a porpoise, I paddle
in battle to brine, ice floes, Pacific
currents, having been spied
stoned and beached in the gavel,
twisted in plastic, cuff-muffled spastic,
the net like unseen gas, thrown back, I gasped
from the bearing to the Bering Sea
over and over and over and over
and over it now, finely, born,
branded purpose bound in blue
emerald, coral to cloud vapor pink, quite,
not quite all over it now, then
bars of dawn frond slide hard
bright deep in the blue storm veil, we touch hear sunspray salt splash,
You/We swimming school
to slide down so low, solo
in a swoon,
to swim in a swim in a swim in a leap
in a swim in a flip in a swim
in a glide in a swim
in a dream to the drums
of foams, curves, spirals,
black light waves together
in adventure.

Rain of the Feminine (Fifth)

They teach us the dance of the very very first rain in years.
They teach us to move.
They leads us to want. They teach us
to run in the rain
and thunder.

Letter to Wind

Listen.

Listen.

Feel again a little. Cool, or cold. Hot and stinging. Feel again the jazz, the burning of clouds in tumbling patterns across the sunset. You are more important to know than statistics. The Word. Talking God. The Breath of Life.

Before thought, before we have begun, the word is, swirling through the hollows, over the dark waters. This is where we come again to the place where birds know how to nest, bees build hives of honey, and geese fly miles and miles and miles north to commemorate chuckling gatherings in the wetlands.

Thank you for my life. I am writing to You, the Wind, for knowing me, for bringing me the water and the rocks from the bottom of the sea, which I have climbed. For stirring the dunes, stinging me into awareness on canyon roads. For worrying the drifts on elegant boulevards in winter. I speak to You, I speak because when I was born, and laughed, You breathed in me. You tickled me awake.

I have known You in many forms in many places; You know Us in all our forms in other places, in collaboration with the whirling world, in felt parody of the pirouette of leaping constellations in slow freaking rapid semblance of what we see as time.

The air we breathe is the air breathed by Trump and Lady Roosevelt, the angels, Emily Bronte, from Annie Dodge Wauneka and Kit Carson, same physical patterns in the lungs and throats of Coretta King and the Endowment for Democracy. And when we are healthy, the air is still free, at large and independent of the empty prophets of Monk and McConnell.

You have shown me rage, the sting and burn of raging incitement of wildfire in injustice and neglect. You have swirled down on dove wings and sat at my window, humming. Because of you the helicopters scream over, overseers in Crips blue, the hummingbirds arrive with monarchs. I will not assimilate to suffocation. I treasure you, run through the answers blowing in the wind in my face.

SECTION FIVE: Birds

Conversation Choirs

When I am a Raven or a Crow, now,
I don't seem to ever want
to go I guess; I get a kick out of
gawking a joke mimicking
scientific intelligence,
pecking at the glass half-full
of matriculating light.

The STOP Sign Meadowlark

Trotting along fast
in a pickup
on the edge
over the curb
through the curve of the willows to
STOP.
Sign says STOP.
I STOP.
Now I hear you, little yellow meadowlark. Hear you
up there playing where
I could have been
still, silhouetted
Superman or the yellow Fairy Godmother.

Cracking the window,
letting in the wind, rolling down by hand
the hardened glass,
hanging out over the wheel, the driver's side
to listen again,
Mozart in a meadowlark,
to peer back up. I can step out
dew petals in the meadow under my bare feet,
and go on back,
or do to put the pedal to the metal under my boot,
floor it and go on.

Improv in a Recovery Café[10]

"We are only potentially apple until we apple;
but we have been always apple."

All I ever wanted was to be a player
of bass clarinets and pianos.
All I ever wanted was to be a lover of you, my own,
a sculptor in soapstone.
All I ever wanted was to be effective,
professionally competent,
never mad activist with a billing code,
that pale yeller with a male diagnosis.
I did not want to be German,
Norwegian, Black, Diné, British, Irish or Blackfoot.
All I ever wanted was to be the Paint whisperer,
a public speaker, a collegiate coach,
an architect of museums and homes,
a glider pilot of the winds and clouds and thermals,
a legislator of the world.
All I ever wanted was to be a grand mother.
I could never be.

We're nothing until smashed in ceramic design
of sacrificial ritual in burning pyre.
I could never be nothing
but a syllabic workaholic honkytonk player
or a story-teller poet;
Want me to draw you a tune of the blues,
long as we're here so late,
drunk with exhaustion and nearly alone?

---

10   www.recoverycafenetwork.org

Mocking Bird Moon

A hefty melody of birdsong
lay on me a beauty of knowing so strong
I was rolled down silly, trilling, thrilling
me, murmuring me, baby, in
bonny Fire. Seared,
scared, stared down by the mockingbird moon, I rocked in raucous
compositions of exquisite
disturbance of bright round burn
of want in a night so long
I would love any ornithologist
who could scrub the music
from the song
hurting so bad this morning.

The Black and White Paint

My Yamaha lifts her delicate head, ears flickering forward,
nickering the warm dark of two dreams.
                    "Gee!" she neighs, begging her long side against
         my hands. I am paint, appaloosa, quarter horse, meant to gallop
along the benches in the canyons, through dawn yellow rippling
kinetics running in red waves wedged between the stolid stone.
And you, meant to ride, who are you, when
I have not been exercised in days in days and hours of years?
         Take the mane, unbridle the blues
         To play , play, to listen to prints, glisten
in sworls of heart to me hear you weep in broken confusion.
She sits me up, testing the ground, the chords in the rains,
         the measure to key the break in lilac from beginning to spring,
         trotting up along the pedals to "Remember you in who I am
along our rocksky winddawn sharp. Flat. Andante, sustain a
mind in a running a little longer, violets in hold to let
the yellow, Rainbow," blues streaming cobalt in "Eeeeee!!!" melody
  beyond the ears flat in flight to Black Mountain,
         necks strong and long in settling rhythm, "AAAAEH"
         Apache Tears and yellow teeth, the me becoming
Lecheguila Cave of whirling rave astroloGEEEE, miner
  the bench, note, the yellow heat, the beat, the streaming
         baby Major! Be mine to know me now, you harken
         never lone me, never alone now, never again alone now,
nobody you and nobody me without the impulse
in the muscle, tune, tone, touch, jump, groan now
         me along to home now!" to heel and wheel and heal
         for a minuet, the minute, the spoken note feel
in the key to know now whinny in the how
we why the cry we live to feel.

Great Grandmother Poetry

What is poetry, anyway?

A great grandmother- why would've they left Norway,

for New York?; same blizzards, same bottomless fiords of inscrutable asphalt,

same taciturnity, fish heaving a last flop in the bins?

She is Poetry, running from the Vikings, the Danes and Swedes to end up in the blizzard

of Nebraska, bereft of Spruce stands and Viking tales

or beeswax. How does somebody sit to write? Is she so phenomenally unique,

flowing from so many pens and keys?

Forgetting the Poem must be like forgetting...

forgetting... Do vowels come first? Is that a cow on top of the sod house?

Or is the meter anapest? Was it proper,

allusion to illusion; did the little girl let the tears out on the prairie?

Fingers dry and caked from too many

udders and too many cobs,

like the palms of aunt and mother?

Should blank verse be blocked, a square quilt, or enjambed/

indented for patterns of the Ten-point Star?

Who sowed the cotton for calico and gingham dresses?

Who is Poetry? How much is okay to know

in labor, in drowning or in wearing white lace? How many

texts are stashed in trunks

with a corn husk doll under the eaves; does it matter

who slept here

beside one sepia photo

of a threshing machine,

boots without laces

and fourteen solemn, too serious, faces;

where even the expression of the dog

desolates?

My Native Language

"Naked mole rats can't write signs for starlings."

Being extremely different than you, different
yet calling myself intelligent and good may be frightening for you.
Your smart PH of THEE image of wholeness as
fitted, sweet, straight, might not be
the picture I have in my mind for me...
I need vastly different patterns to survive.
Living my dangerous, avoid it;
weird little nerd, piggy and crooked,
struggling through bewildering slime and limestone,
riding hot columns of crystal monsters.
Might be poison for you and a potluck for me.
They'd kill you, but they are home to miners.

Taters'll drown in a pool of exotic anemone.
We look the same in parts and pieces,
But a cat ain't a catfish, and a pony ain't a porpoise;
some strive, some dive, and some thrive
in a freeze of heaving sea.

Some kids are polyester presentation,
and some of these kids are cacti.
Some are meant for plain, others for the rare.
My native language might win your war.
Don't kill the woods from your comfort zone,
planting my dunes like you like your meadow.
Don't assimilate and enculturate
to abandon, disorder or deprive us because
you cannot understand why we're not white, red or blue.
Wait for the curators and the connoisseurs to enlighten you.
Free us to care for our own.

Composition Mentor

"One day I heard a fire bell. Instead of crying out and hiding, I rushed to the piano and tried to reproduce the sounds." —Nadia Boulanger[11]

You don't get notes of oak
in chardonnay, the honey; theory of the music,
harangued and banged
with no give, no village you want
to love to life, and no vibrato,
bringing in bucks, sanging, wronging
in stages of decomposition, concert of a
consort of the clanging symbol.
Let yourself go onto the scary flats once, freed of freedom,
splriiinlinngling the strings, hearing
addiction, the deprivation
in an abandoned chest
of treasure, the measure,
the siren song call, babycry-wise
lullaby in the syllabi, forgivin,
the misty,
the improv, the risky,
the frisky, the try.
a choired co-op in embodied instruments,
not wood or brass but tissue and organ of sinuous resilience.
She lets you know, you know.
Lays her beau down
to bow in the harmony to fill in the rest.

---

11   Quincy Jones' composition professer in Paris

Poetic Redemption

Wisdom is
free as water, as words, as the land upon which we dwell,
the dope de hope-hope
hip-hop language foreign and domestic, the mope, the bombs,
bringing home the bacon, beer and bread and soap on a rope,
cooks and janitors dropping in, dropping out to shriek like light jets and
eagles,
muttering spin over rolling the logs,
happy grandpas yelling over the crazy dogs, all
the little kids, administrative assistants, National Guard
out your doors and out your windows -

Well, you hear all day then - NICE me some of that poetry!
They never taught Nice at my school...
Show me the music and math in the poetry. I'd do anything to study better
than statistics for accounting and making bombers,
propaganda for empirical history,
or greater-than compliance for responsibility.

Tell me the joke to doing the checkbook.
They never taught elegant communication at my
school...
Somebody said I might be a quick study;
couldn't you home me some of them beautiful words,
sit on your porch (I'm awful tired),
just coach me to empty the scraps
and empty the trash again, to see the forgiveness in empty trash
and to empty the trash tomorrow.
You got a toilet to wash, I'll scrub it out
to be let in the House. Just teach me
cleanup and laundering the poetry.

Ha!? Well, might as well wash me now, bathe me, shower, shampoo and squeak my hair,
and comb and brush and comb and hush,
                        hush... brush until its shiny, accepting the sob
        to get over the cry. You really might could home me the stanza then.

                                Teach me molasses and cook your juicy peach
                compote, oatmeal with nuts and tiny chunks of chocolate.
        Spoonful the sugar with that shit-bit medicine; yeah, I'll take
                        your damn poetry again! AGAIN!
                                        Ok! All Right! Again, Wha?!

        Then look at me, that's New Me sitting there at the table
gluing paperscraps and syllables
                                together for books, because you made me
                some hot, hot sweet and lime-sour poetry.

        See me and get me slow, to stop, to detail the story on stage,
"Safe with me now, Hey, Little Son Shine, here in the telling."
                (Rock and talk without restraints but rhymes).
        Poetry don't take no private insurance, just a walk in the park of I Ams
                with the analog experience in listening to time.
                        I'll run on and play to leave you alone, promise not to fight
        or bully the pitbull to bite, or lose your
                                home to talk talk talk and psychotropics
or rehab methadone, desperate addicted to the Institute of Poetry.
                Coach the satisfaction in crack
                of the bat on a ball and not a brain
                and how, oh, JESUS CHRIST!, to Run! Run! Run!
                Run! Run! and Sliiiiiiide! SAFE! Home!!!!!
        Scream me that "Yeah, Yeah, Yeah, Girl!" poetry!

We Thought They Took Our Music

"They wanted the medicine of the music
without the rest and wisdom music loves."

They ached for our nurtured gardens, cultured lives; then
they wiped them out.
We thought they took our world, but they didn't, but we thought so.

They came on down as the sun went down shrieking, smiling
out of grim grins in the red of the sunset behind them in a blaze,
and they took away our sins, our hearts, our loves, and our animism,
and joy in animation to worship their father in their independent nation.
We thought they took our hearts, but they didn't, but we thought so.

For our own good, they took our children to rape and raise,
they took our elders to stick in glass boxes in museums and chrome rooms for research,
they took our healers and shook them up and made
them honored wives and taught them to be men.
We thought they took our kindness, but they didn't, but we thought so.

They shot the shamans and wiped our medicine women from memory in celebratory bonfires
convicted as criminals or contagious. If we were ashamed or terrified, enraged or confused
they sold us
a pharmaceutical fortune for labwork and a digital diagnosis.
We thought they took our minds, but they didn't, but we thought so.

They paid us dead wages for teaching and nursing and mending their kids
that we should *feel* fulfilled.
They thought they took our words, but they didn't but they thought so.

They traded us, made us, laid us, like them made for goodness.
We thought they took our villages, but they didn't;
we've found each other again.

Thin Blue Line [Sky II]

"It is not a teeter totter; it is a solitary flight
in the gyrating labyrinth; and sometimes it goes on in space
for years. And sometimes what we learn becomes useful."

Mind in solitary confinement,
never forget your Sky. Remember his lullaby.
If never have you have been held in his gray flannel pajamies,
buy an electric jolt out of the digital beep. Go deep. Go high!
You want to fly. Take off in a quiet cabin to find him.
Sky is not lost until you are in him.
Click "LIKE" on Sky in a vapor roll, haughty cold
comedy caucus of political parrots on a telephone poll,
his dark who of moaning sigh,
that shifty tuneless "Ain't No Sunshine" whistling by.

Love the Sky, those sexy blues
of familiar feather-fluttering deep in the belly
slap of easy breezy in coy caprice,
snow-cones and peaches up in the ruffles;
then follow the feeling, follow your bliss in
the muffle, the pickup, the hiccup, the curve to the arc
to scream in a long whine down to the shine,
white-petal edge of the cumulo-nimbus cloud! Wheee...
Why, if you are lost in a fog, remember Sky,
grey flapping, flap, flap hot, dark,
pink, corn-pollen dirt in yellow,
crimson cactus-flower lover of the loony moon
in your own holy-wind white of cobalt blue

Who will always be part of the world
Who loves you...

Rain of the Feminine (Sixth)

We want to twist again like little brown
eagles in little eggs; we want to wiggle
and peck; to see what's out there. We want to remember
how it was to grow or wait; we want to fight
like bean sprouts up out of the ground,

we want to know, we want to stretch,
we need to be educated, have babies,
or not, or drive to Chicago
in pockets of glass, or stay home.

Letter to Consciousness

You, old young One, are the oldest and the new beginner. You are the hardest and the easiest Teacher. When I sit with You, I don't know if You want to play or pontificate in this moment. What if we did not know where we are going? You contemplate grasshoppers. You sit at the well and chat with ladies who are not pillars of civic duty. You tell Your disciples to go back and meditate another fourteen years in a cave. You gently wash your twins on top of the mesa. You have told me over and over and over, "I can help you, if you just show up. Be with Us."

John Trudell said once in the circle that the women said to the men, "Stand and fight! Our children will die without warriors!" And so they fought, at Alcatraz, the BIA Gallery and at Wounded Knee. But what Trudell said later was what they lacked was that no one stopped to think. We have one sense: Sight. We have one elder: Gold. And so we are blind beggars, thrashing about with canes and scepters. We have come to believe we know everything. And so we are stupid.

Why collaborate with injustice and self-enslavement? Funding is not a substitute for creation. Action without the preparation in the Beauty Way, the Beatitudes, is wasted energy. Restore villages with the business networks of mothers. Action is the life-blood of activism. There can be a breathing in the separate urgencies in rhythm between the male and the female. Intelligence is simply the communication through storytelling between the mind, the muscle and the emotion. It cannot be done without children, hummingbirds, bees, time, strings of neurons and free shared transportation systems.

I do not ask dissemblance or anarchy. You are so proud of the brutality with which you treat yourselves and your college students. I ask for peace, patience, and to leave us alone already. Do not send the Cavalry in Red Coats or the Missionaries in Blue. Send traders and teachers by invitation only. Let the mothers and the aunties work with our men and those who are of the alchemy of these. I beg you stop. Maybe history is told by the victor, but maybe the war can be over. Maybe we are not in a war at all, but in a performance on a stage with an audience of ancestors and aliens. Maybe renaissance happens in lounge chairs, barns, bedrooms and garages, in gentleness, in softness and breathing in both fire and water, both rock and wind, both empty space and the fullness of consciousness. This is All.

SECTION SIX: Wild Horses

My Paints

My Mares, painted red, spotted white,
always will resent your average
picky yellow nips on our rumps, but we
just keep running along, galloping to be
galloping sometimes, loving
the lathering in the winds on the flattops,
crazy in communion with the fillies
in the rich pink glass of frost in the grass.

Leah, Artist in a Box on Grande Avenue

*"You cannot pay the I Are US and the I AM
with two sides of the same dollar bill"*

The design, the song, the fine art
of conversation Is the soft and sting of early snow,
green-blue bubbles flailing in a bathtub of little blondes
held down by the backs of the neck
by the scared scarred bony memories of the father,
the seven-year old with her forced abortion cross of freeways across the belly
of the landscape, down the navel into the crevasses
of the soft petal pink womb of the muted feminine. The furor is not Love,
and not your father. Oh, don't give me that metaverse of the
railroad track through a project with a gold mine;
kids playing on a dirt curb with FDA-approved Fentanyl and Seroquel,
mother working for health at the drugstore counter,
church with a lock on the door and a Sunday bookstore,
father paid in shame or fame and gasoline,
sisters tortured in border boot camp for freedom of the homeland
gauche security, that business of insurance for elder convalescence,
for half-life in a backlot cancer studio of lye and broken
asphalt... Life is not a cache;
Caesar's earn is twenty bucks of paper ash.
Art is not only all about the money, honey,
only the hunt, the shop, the mortgage,
only books and a bathroom, a penthouse and a limo,
only billboards, badges and autographs,
marketing, and packaging,
only a cook and a caretaker, casket on credit,
only rocket science shellack or the Nobel Prize...
Art is not a frame, the fame, a muse of paint or process, only;
art is all about the lonely.

The Dancer's Father

There was this little Russian dancer they called a "white crow"
                                        because he wasn't really quite like the others.

        When White Crow's father came home
                from the wars, he marched that little boy
        out to the woods,
                        built a tiny campfire to leave Rudolph Nureyev there huddling
                howling with the wolves.

                                Why'd that daddy soldier to do that?
                Maybe all that soldier knew was terror.
        And maybe that soldier daddy did not want that boy to end up
                in a maze of a muddy puddle like his old army buddies in the trenches.
                Maybe all that daddy
                        soldier saw anymore was a bloody haze.

                And salvation,
        having come home from the war to that beautiful delicate lively kid.
But I don't want to be an army tank anymore, clanking this tonnage
                                        through somebody's bloody ruts,
        some old lady's meadow, blowing up villages, blasting
        shrapnel and bullets at anything that moves.

Military tanks can be dangerously brutal
                        to clean up, I've found.
                        But if I ever get it done, I'm gonna bury my
        green machine in roses and little kids
                to cruise every Friday night down the Boulevard
                                in a company of fifty loco lowriders.

Art and Sole of a Boot

I guess here it is, a galaxy of goozhé,
rich, almost red in its brownish, old whole-wheat crushed pie crust
texture unrolled, depressed, pretty
stinky, on an uncooked sidewalk....

The whole design campaign of a Size-14 thought:
Entrances prop the heel,
the pride organic to the toes,
shoelaces probably begun by technical pencil on graphite paper, rulers

in a glass office over Dubai most certainly seen from close to the top,
no doubt a Director of Graphics fresh out of the Chicago Institute of Art,
chumping more pot stickers than she ever did Cheetos,
trying to make sure she drinks enough
store-bought water every day.
She designed this boot sole to sell.
Would she see my plaque as archetypal?
The simple aesthetic is flawless,
the brightness, well-rounded and thick and evocative
and nasty.
The breeze is slight, white. It usually is, here in Highland Park,
stirring memories of yellowy ginkgo biloba under
the awning of Fashion 21 and Slow Culture.

Somebody worked awful hard.
The shit's absolutely flawless.
Somebody needs to take the design of it home.

I guess this is that, then, what
a motorcycle boot sole can do
to a commemorative medallion in bronze
Husky poo.

<u>*Therese, Artist in a Box on Broadway*</u>

Sitting pretty on Broadway
right downtown on a long walk of the cold hard truth, hanging ropes with a whole lot of safety pins
I got stuck in a hem in a wool skirt I got in the alley in the Fashion District,
and yellow yarn, cotton threads and macrame, sewing, knotting, hiding in a cardboard condo
refrigerator box draped duct tape on garbage bags,
tying up the loose ends out of the rags with a crochet needle I bought at the Mission,
running like a rat from the cold hard truth from another Arts District Sanitation.
"NO... EBT!" "NO... Credit!" And the sign on that door says, "NO....
Public Restrooms!" EBT ain't free. They hate me.

Guards at the fountains say, "No..." dipping in a water bottle, taking a bath or cooling your feet
in the beautiful river they stole from the Navajo. Never seemed a citizen of the
united States where I was born,
genetic of the Trail of Tears, the Great Depression, Oklahoma to Chicago to San Diego back...
Sign on the school says, "NO... foreign language spoken here!" You can't talk Choctaw,
but you can pontificate in British!
Somebody stole your land for a church and a culture clash, your home
is a box, "Thou Shalt Nots" and yarns in gerrymandering maps from the mission.
In how many other little cities with Second Street tunnels have women hidden in a run
to find help? Sign says, "NO..." "NO shirt, NO shoes, NO service..." "NO... Cash!" "NO... Exit!"
And "NO... Liberty, EBT and NO public restrooms!"

Father paid off to die for freedom of the Homeland; Irish, Black, White Trash and Choctaw.
Abandoned by a battered mom,
and the paper said, "NO...
and the paper said NO...,
and the paper said NO...,
rejection becomes your soul.
Ain't got a family, you ain't got a country; too sick to work and you ain't wealthy?
Well, then you ain't got a dentist or a PPO! (They going to call *me* crazy.)
And the sign on the door says, "NO..." Can't be here! You ain't healthy!

And no, them meds in the bottle ain't medicine, that's
coma compliance, sit down shut up science
study of finance, dead elephants and humans in cages.
(You kind of gotta BE a dancer to study a dancer.)

Careful never to let anybody know you; slow. Slow, thoughtful, careful.
Don't show. Just sew! Just so! Just sow! Just so!
They'll steal, as they done tried and stole my soul. They might arrest me;
they took my sexy. Didn't get my sense, though;
honey, I'd show you in a tapestry if you sit on the cold hard truth with me with
a Quarter Pounder with Cheese and a five dollar bill,
all my yarns and blues and greens from Goodwill,
hours and hours and hours on the Fourth of July, hours and hours in a cold shower in November,
a giant plastic hook looks like silver,
not so hard to hold, and not so hard to slide into the pattern and bring through.
An artist in the studio and an artist in a box are both a genius in a rent-free room.
At night I slide my studio in Prussian Blue
against the warm brick wall to crawl back deep in my gallery of pretty beads,
trusty box cutter, pepper spray, shit bucket,
bottle of water and macrame and a wig like Marilyn Monroe.
You lose it all, you can do three things: I can think, I can sew, and I can fast...
Oh, I could wait; but you try sleeping on the cold hard truth with the cops,
"sanitation department" and a billion greedy bed bugs!
What is a tiny house village, anyway? Looks like a fort or a kennel to me.
"No tipis, travelers, campers or gypsies." Please, can I *have* your family,
a college degree in insanity, rat race of debt, two-day vaca,
a doctor cares more about quality of life than "quality of the patient,"
rent that makes sense for stolen property?

They're coming to take me to court for the last things I got:
my needles, the wind, the sun, my mind, my liberty or death, and I got more stories than Star Wars,
but, "NO!"
Sign on my box says, "NO..." bright duck tape red. Dare you! See that?, sign on the box says, "NO."
"NO Liberty, EBT, and NO public restrooms." EBT ain't free. They hate me.

Noticing a Goose

I saw a dead goose. It was a goose.
And it was dead.
            I guess I should ask the priest is a dead goose a goose?
      She sported quite a nice bill,
            as any goose would, curvy...
                  cool Erte fashion
                        in sassy black and white feathers
                              and pretty clawed toes.

      She'd broke her back,
            nesting in a congregation of ants, stained bottle glass staring
                  and silk remnants of red rags.

A femme promenaded past with her baby
                  pugs fairly ecstatic about the finding of a rare
      real goose on the walk.
The goose does not fit along a lakeside feathering
            dirty dainty sprays like a gown of chiffon in Vogue...
Drivers in killer cars groan outside her Parisian pillars;
      riding never farther forward
                  than their dash and text
                        in air-conditioned upholstered
                              pews, set back straight
            deprived, unaware that here
      was, in MacArthur Park, in her final emigration,
                  a beautifully feathered goose.
            There was.

Maurica, Artist in a Box on Hope

"Dead people don't bleed."

Cutting is the opposite of death by artificial intelligence;
cutting through the falsies of a plastic Barbie Doll in a Hope Street green screen of virtual
reality, accounting in an oak box buried a plot in the office.
(She does not want to cut, She doesn't want to cut, She doesn't want to bleed anymore)
As a number, a plastic fern on the furniture, algorithm in ink for statistical dots (doodling drops
in the margins), in a cul-de-sac cubicle bank tower on the twenty second floor, wounds
in the eyes, under ankle stockings, between the knuckles, inside the tender skin
of the elbows, raw, and high up on the wrists bound
in bandages, infected, raw, tucked, wrapped... Bleeding makes abandonment bearable;
someone punished for leaving her, through bloodlet and daily sacrifice. They won't notice;
they don't see her,
tracking the strokes of her fingers, her IP address, her badge, her screen,
her face when she goes to the bathroom or talks out loud, Location, Location, Location, hiding in
Polynesian etchings of razors, broken glass, can lids, needles in her skin.
Bleeding is a 'me too movement' of the rape of a muffled child,
the opposite of drugs and no less dangerous,
when she doesn't even need the mess, sticky and stench behind a Maybelline veil,
the sharp glass, red wine under a napkin at a soiree reception
for the wedding of an old boyfriend.
Bleeding is rejection of rejection, the artwork of personal advocacy and activism.
What's else is there? Sit down. Shut up. Sit up. Be a good girl.
Restrain the pain in a psychotropic? Be proper. Pretend.
And SMILE. SMILE! "Hello, sir, may I help you?"
No, Baby! Paint! In crimson! Talk about it! Write it in granite! Or find a partner!
And CRY! Cry, "Please, can you help me?"
Cry! Scream! Love! Dance! Roar!
You do not have to bleed, infected with pain, strangled in shame;
It was not your fault or destiny of genetics.
You don't have to cut anymore.

I Am My Body

I am my body, and will not be dictated to.
I am my eyes and will not
                          be dictated to by what I see in a glass,
          in the neon museum of my eyelids or on TV.
I am my ears and I will not be dictated to by the heartthrob
                          on the radio, smoozhing jazz in the soul along to belonging snuggy
          in the pillow or charging up the dawn to fine. I'm fine.

I am the crown point of my mind,
                          and will not be dictated to by a bony skull or scary purple hairdo;
I snub the stub of the toe.
I am my voice and will not hold my tongue or baby it.
                          Huh, are you kidding me? I suffer, you suffer, let's just suffer together forever!
I am my right mind and will not be dictated to by reason
                          of the left brain or by the frightful yelling in the haul.
I am my hypothalamus in the middle
          of my dream, not to be managed by the hippocampus or the paltry pineal
                          gland that is so unscientifically slow,
          or that wild, reptile child unmentionable amygdala out back.
And I am my left lung and will never be swayed by the right,
                          my perverse abdominals independent of the smelly gut, the greasy liver,
                          a delicate toleration of the filth.
I am my beautiful roses of nipples always hidden
                                    though never protected or cherished in shame.
I am my womb. My womb. A womb of my own,
                          a studio. And I will not be dictated to,
or hidden in a name, this, my blood is real, crimson, bloody, sticky as clay slip, acrylic paint
          and epoxy, it will not be ignored or pretended away, unthought, unfelt, unnoticed
                    unlearned in books and universities,
          unstudied, unacknowledged, unmentioned because it is unique to my gender.

I am a long proactive organ, the courageous nerve of me
                        that's free of that long stack of wacky scaredy bones or lazy muscle
        at the back. I am my vagina and will not be moved by anybody else I choose
                        to come to play, no matter
            how they move, how hefty, happy, hot or urgent.
                            Er... well... maybe,

        but I am my thick resilient skin and will not be dictated to
        by somebody's bourgeois fashion sin in color or design, not affected by sticks,
afflicted by stones, a bath of easy breezy burning embers of the long slow sigh...down
                        from the temple to
        the delicate nape of the neck rolling
                        over wet round
                            muscley warm in a drippy
                                tickle to the tickle
            in the arch... hmmmm... er, help, oh...
I am my strong legs that got me here so far, and I will not be dictated to
                by the weakness of the knees, the hardness of the walk, the wood
        of the stage or the air of the dance. I am my lap and will not be dictated to
        by the bony wiggling of silly kids begging comedy or mysteries or a check for the
                broken plate glass, their wide excited eyes in the bright hope of their lives.
I am my heart and will not be dictated by contractions of this problematic throb
                        of love for all of you.

I am my soul and I will not be dictated to by the moon,
                the scriptures or the smothering of my breath. I am my eyes and will not be
        dictated to by anything I see. You see? I am my soul. I am my body, I am my mind.
I am Myself. I am my body and will not be dictated to by you. Me!
                        Me, Me, Me, Me, Me! And
                    I Am
            perfectly, perfectly free.

You're Never So Lost

You are never so lost as when they find you.
I grew up curled in the house of White Shell Woman;
but I never knew.

Stay away from the oil company roads or you can be
violently ejected;
Hide inside the boulders and branches or be raped and rejected;
Stay away from the sheep; they're run by giant dogs.

I was in the Womb, safe in the home of the juniper of dawn,
clear and soft in the winding words across her deerskin shoulders
until I was told to come down.

There's no safety on the flat of the
desert;
you are never so lost as when they find you.

You are never so lost as when they find you, woman
before I was a little girl,
old woman in a shoe, so many children didn't know what to do.
You could never get those kids to stop
howling,
growling in bellies that grew and grew;
They wait, they watch,
but you can't get 'em through.

You're never so lost as when they find you.

You're never so lost as when they find you; you can be shot in the face
                    by the Taliban for saying what you think you saw
          and live to address the united nations;
                         or shot down by a church on Facebook for clearing your throat;
     the comeback's slow, up over
                         the bleeding lip of the edge where they ask and ask
          and ask you where you been?

I've been in the home of White Shell Woman; they say the Mesa starts to see you
          the minute you return to notice
               the brawn of the bows
                    in waves of sage,
                         the prisms,
                              the storms,
               the sparkle in the dark
                    flow of her yellow skirts in the wind,
                    the blackened stone in the freeze
                    in the eyes of wise men,
                         the weave of epic flames,
               the folds of hides in the white behind her.

     Well, you've climbed down to me too
          in the wash, through that little crack.
                    You see I see you now, but I find myself
          tossed and never so observed,
                    lost in your eyes of thought, so regarded
          or present as when
                    you find me.

125

Rain of the Feminine (Seventh)

We are cold from the rain and bent from the strain,
sore, hoarse, bruised and ecstatic.
We are hot, so hot and alive in the minute, bright
shells exploding all around us, we see each other
struggling,
spinning,
writhing,
giggling
and not stuffed inside
anymore.

Letter to the Divine

You are best known as the Breath of the Word, the light space of the unknown One we only come to know in gratitude and awareness, as Truth, as Beauty, as Goodness. You hold the six elements together, the fulcrum and still point in the vortex. You are Temperance, Balance.

Without an infinity of understandings, we come back to you, to feel, to rest. We come back. We come back. We sit and adore Your adoration of us, the simplicity of our blind struggle. We see darkly in a glass through the metaphor, "This is That."

I thank You from the bottom of Your Heart. You hold me. You hold us, whether or not we rest in the holding, to strengthen to dance in Your performance.

SECTION SEVEN: Bees

Neurons, Organs and Minds

When ten thousand bees come in from
playing in the flowers, what'd we do now?
They say we're dying, but I still hear the buzz
in the plumeria, in the lilacs and the jasmine.
There is plenty of room in the universe
for particles to produce
one twelfth of a teaspoon of honey in a lifetime.

Particles are waves.
What do we do as
little things gathering to hive in a village?
I'm tasting a little honey and
feel a little better today. Maybe I'll live.
And you might too.

The Natural Nectar

The mountain flames; its fire comes
from somewhere. Goes
somewhere.
The tree is apple; its sugar comes
from somewhere. Goes
somewhere.
Creation is the taste, the sup,
the sip, the touch, the intake jerk
talk of the Conscious blank stare of exposure
to vanilla, serial killer, shock, orgasm or wasabi.
Resurrection.
You can always call the Creator who made you to heal you;
(it might not be obvious if you don't pay attention.)
We don't express ourselves; we reflect the glass we live in.
You can't teach water.
You cannot teach gold or mushroom,
medicine or honey,
but you can bring it home.
Art dances down to the crowded lobby
to welcome you to Windsor; all that belongs
to your Beloved belongs to you now, rich
in Love with Life now,
the Desire that through the melting tubes
spirts crimson fire,
the Force that through the green fuse
drives the fruit, the flow,
the Joy that through the wound
brings life as sacrifice.

<u>*One Phoenix Family*</u>[12]

The Phoenix
rises,
feathers glittering with fire,
charred blood scaling from his breast.
Lifted from the ashes (I am free,
I am free!)
"Oh, look at me!"
He is
crying.

Rising
red from the smoldering fragments, the mother bird is looking down.
"Oh, lookee you, you beautiful little things,
just look at those soppy feathers,
those cute little knobby claws!"

(Oh, goochee, goochee!
Hang on. I got to fly. Before you wake,
I'll be back.)

This is what
she is muttering
happily.

---

12   I am here exploring the idea that the feminine principle in human nature — whether in families, villages, organizations or national leadership - is not identical to the masculine; that it consists in loving observation (presence), firm interaction (personal immediate response), and the collaboration of associations of groups. Wherever the feminine principle is disrespected, deleted, or assimilated, civilization collapses into totalitarianism and civil war.

"En Medio Tutisimus Ibis"

"It is always better to walk the middle course." —Aristotle

Where can you find a tuner with a good ear and a fork?
Melody. Strung out, restrung, long, aligned,
text to textile tapestry, tap
tap tap hum-type rung,
the weft taught in a caught in a thought, felt,
the bridled tongue shout out electric warpwoven
run again and over and over again before
three cups of Columbian.
Kneel before the jury, might be the last time you got your head
in your fingers on chords, harmony, pop song destitution of
a destination, to trust the sour, the too
sweet, the tweet, the loose, Not, or the rotten
tomato, long as you're paying attention.
Opera, quilt block, formal equation,
mountain passes, the rich
stitch witchery in strung piano wire, the zzzzzzzzz vibe
in the wave in the ultrasound, the straight, the variation,
wild comeback power modulation: changing the bulb
in the medical gaslight for gracenotes in the librettro.
History and education is a straightedge architectural rendering on
how characters are supposed to, SHOULD,
hang out over the stage.
and swing...
whine Nessun Dorma...
And climb down later for the dime,
the dinner, and the wine,
intact.

Sacred Heart Hospital Chapel

She was dying.
So I hung in the nave with a votive flame in hope that
the Madonna would feel me, starving for the spiritual intelligence
to be in that communion, praying not to be distracted by taxicabs
or a clackety rash of tourists at the back...
I mean, what if I missed Them?,
the Pieta, what if They revolved round like marble Disney dummies on a cathedral merry-go-round,
the Mother grasping the naked limp limbs of the battered Christ,
white eyes passing my dark visions of revolution and rebellion...? What if I missed
like the billy goats of revelations Their forgiveness...?
But, no, They sat tight a minute, scanning. Me. Looking up,
looking down, disturbed.

Shatter of breezy luminaries, irreligious laughter clatter high
platforms, tourists bowing lowing obeisance, surround sound at the rail like a veil,
male knuckles, nails polished, girl cheeks,
incense of jersey icons on T-shirts, new denim, hot breath, beanies, Ray Bans in the murk,
with a mini poodle, cotton candy magenta, jostled and joked.

Virgin with a God in her lap and a Mona Lisa grin, in observance, fire nodding grim with gold lashes
beautified saints in silicon.
An old-man hand with the marble-like skin of the high class,
handed me a hanky, stained,
embroidered with MM, or HEF, or SR, or MF, or OP or CS, or SG or I don't know,
glass running over, holy ghost seen through cataracts of crystal iconography god is.
Energy, Synergy. Linen. Live. Love. Life. Warm.
And sticky. And snotty. And real.
And wet.

The Pollinator Profession

"Poetry is music. And nothing but music. Words with musical emphasis." —Amari Baraka

Funky old Poets, that you see me makes me,
old bumbling honey bee,
clicking batons across the board of blooming matriculation through
propellers of pinkening right along a tickle on a stamen,
"Write on, ride on." I work-shopped you today. You heard me.
You saw me today. I read you there.
Involuntary action of golden pollen to honey gold to go to work tomorrow. A moment...
a balance
on wind rumble be-ruffling purpling pronounced over the broadcast mean
screened masks over it all the byting,
in twitter and zoom of springing community gardens,
tanka train SCReech and trashcan clash
smashed down like Coke cans in long cool green muse-ical medical miracle
haul of vision viral galactical hohum tactical lattice chokework of the buzz, still, honey heavy
busy dizzy buzz baby blue. Just saying, saying/playing bright mum cloud
to meme, quote to haiku.
No commercial bee, freebee. Only me and All write, baby sup worship to seedling
to sapling
to trunk
to limb
to bud
to orange and almond apple blossom rewinding the minding inner force
pounding in a bump in the sap slide down turn-style delicate
courage in cream, beeing enthralled,
stalled stubborn new nut, blue deans, thunder boom sweet cool in shady wait
elongated
in lightening.

My Kitchen Sink

"The arterial Zen of matriarchal artcraft, the kingdom of God within you."

The water is warm. A storm is coming in; pretty soon, I'll need
to call the children. The dishes in my sink belonged to my
grandmother, lilacs and cream, made in U.S.A., the silver given to
my mother on her wedding day. I am wet nearly to the elbows;
the water so warm. The sky is heavy out beyond the shed. Those
kids you'd think would know when to come in out of the cold.
They think they can play forever.

I love this kitchen sink. I've canned pickles and beets, scrubbed
potatoes. We sanitize the Bell jars; we husk the corn, we shuck, we
wash the corn. We boil the jars. From the big bowls in the sink, we
spoon silos of kernels into the jars to be boiled in vats of hot water,
counseling the men and the kids passing through, tormenting
themselves on the aroma of homemade wheat rolls and oyster corn
pudding. Snowflakes float in the window, slow; they say this may be
a big one. The grandkids play with the ponies by the barn;
I'll call them in soon.

My sink holds a turkey; every year, the biggest turkey we ever
raised. I am grateful for the sacrifice. Neddy plucks it, lowers the
giant bird into the roaster in the sink for me to carefully wash,
tossing the entrails in an ice-cream bucket for the hogs. Firm
liver, plump and reddish brown. I set aside the heart, the gizzard,
the neck and the liver for giblet gravy, I massage the turkey skin
with butter cream, garlic, salt, pepper, basil, parsley, and honey.
Harold helps me lift the roaster down to the oven.

Belinda was fourteen when she told us she was pregnant, the
only Thanksgiving I remember silence at the table. She helped
me wash up after, the water so warm, forgiving, hopeful with
beautiful dishes with lilacs, clear sturdy glasses, curved handles
on the coffee cups. Every speck I feel in my fingers as I wash.
The cotton-woods are swaying in rising wind;
it's about that time to call the children.

My sink is my business. Twice a week, I separate the milk
from the cream for selling to the neighbors. Harold takes
the milk to the cooler in the milkhouse
for the truck to come by to pick up.

Now I am going to wash Addy, my newest, my precious great
granddaughter. She has suffered so much. Her joints are off
balance, so she fusses. I hold her in the warm water with the
crook of my arm to wash her fine skin. Pressing my cheek to hers,
we coo and smile. The water is warm. I place her on a fluffy towel
to carefully rub her body; she winces slightly; she smells clean;
she whimpers; she turns her head to sleep.

Oh, my. The sky is deep blue-gray. I pull the plug from the sink. The
water was warm; I dry my hands on a clean cotton towel.
Those kids have all got to come in, right now.
I'll ring the bell...

Promised Land

Looking for a new world, this one's done; hey, you happened to seen the promised land?
Ever been there? I've been hunting Google Earth, Scientific American
and Archeology Magazine and I don't see it.
Somebody said it's in Jerusalem or Boston, or West L.A.,
but it's supposed to be Peace. May be a
church, a temple of love, right? They've posited Plymouth Rock, Mecca, London,
the East Indies, the Vatican, Berlin,
Okinawa, Shambhala and the Seven Cities of Cibola, but
everybody living there says it's someplace else.
Some say state of mind or Kingdom of God, eternal Nirvana, but if it's a land,
couldn't you map it, and if it's a state, real, kind, free, have you ever met Her?

Well, I did, a few times:
turquoise valley in sunrise moon in the snow...
scruffy gray stray with a happy light and a lick...
Mary's warm fingers on my sweaty T-shirt...
flock of raucous feathers white and black...
breath of Heaven Scent...
a fingerprint on a cream pot from the 20's...
guy across from me dark with seagreen eyes and galactic intelligence...
one cold crack in a springblack rock at the end of a hot broke road...

I'm keeping going, but I got to stop, ask, "You seen sign, seen or been to the
promised land, is It steady, gravity, still, or does She dance? Have you been?
And how'd She look, and what'd He seem like, and how long did you get to stay?"
I don't live on bread alone, but grateful every minute
for buddies and the manna
and the hard hardy life in the promised land.

Rez Basketball in Winter Solstice

The center cannot hold
      without the battered leather,
   or without
      the air of the bike pump
           lighter than anything,
   or without
      the gravity of trajectory
         and revolution in the long shot,
           the dunk...
   or whatever that is in communion
         with the balance n' bounce of
           your hot hasty breath
           on the freezing tips of your fingers...
but there might be mini Trinity
      in the common object:
         the thought, the work and the spark,
        the mother, the son and new father
    let swish
      in the pink ice dawn of headlamps
        of the pick-
        up.

Hold My Hands
(An Online Dance Poem)

The first hands I thought were kind were brown, teaching me to pat bread for the
hot fat without burning my hymn piano fingers on a black iron skillet. Her name
was Blanche Juan. But there are no such things as unkind hands; they teach us, with
claws, clay, slaps, waterboarding and coaching about the world in stages.

Hold hands, now, everybody... flower-sanded, palm-polished worn leather fingers,
    filigreed life-lines, knobby gray knuckled
        bent around pan handles-

    -hold my hands-

    patchy ailing pale baby, pink-thin kid skin kneading, the want
        over the wail, tiny teeny weeny grasps of surprise, wine-skins
        moist in saltsheen and Irish cream a few hours old,
          ninety-five today-

    -hold my hands-

        -teeny weeny stillborn fingers under the giant thumb
    of a young mother, named and unnamed,
        you never met, this many years old in Septicember May
graduating high kid gloves to
        her refining elbows, gloss-black
    over the knot of a hidden ring, singing brass
        knuckled hard perseverance-

    -hold my hands-

-Megan Duncan, Cory Cofer, I guess we're really doing this, huh? I feel you
here this morning on the bench at Hacienda of Hope and it minds me how I
used to run down on the Gold Line to Union Station to flash an improv with the
passengers on the public piano down there. It weren't the Keck piano; before the
pandemic it was kept up, tuned. I never got why they'd maintain a train or a CT

*SCAN machine and not a piano; you never heard a five-year old for the first time or
a blues vet like that, side by side but, improv, fresh... it's the goddess moving over
the face of the rippling steel, no matter at Verdugo Hills Geropsyche or Pasadena
Senior Center. She is the gentle intellectual, the potters, Nampeyo and Jean Taylor,
speaks Oriole sign language, for anyone who has the ear to hear Her, yeah?-*

-hold my hands-

-eager dance tonight, own aching, pretty, shaking
                              lively arms this evening long
              as sweet, sixteen, and never been kissed er never bin missed, and here.

-hold my hands-

-patty-cake palms in time, rhyme on mine steady on your waist, handshake
                    dish-pan grand scars of dark ghosts,
                              the missing tip of an index or the end of a limb,
          long elegant flutter of bars of jazz Miles
                    to Corea decedent of Polonaise grace,
                         fresh from hot-steam jars of jalapeno jam,
                    adolescent cool gullibility on a baseball bat, the play sword
                         vision of defense or conquest-

-hold my hands-

-grandfather tool hooks, the bayonette, the badge, the baby,
          the broom, the workgloves, the hammer,
               the wrench, the rifle, the mortar board, metal prosthetic,
                    the cotton washcloth in fragile olive rosemary fingerprints
          brought to purple lips, clapping, clapping stubby, stubborn claws
               like glittering December branches, snowflake melt on the knuckle.
          ...independent in the parking rights at twenty-one years old,
                    his, cold hands
          held, wrapped in comic books or mittens or plaster,
                              fist or the finger,

-hold my hands-

-braced, the wrists, wise black, blistered, bronzed,
pull, holding, heavy handed tug, their tugging,
hugging the firm grip, the shrug of trembling,

-hold my hands-

all hands on deck, strong and empty offering cake... on your tenth birthday tug of war, hold, the immediate touch.

-hold my hands-

-Mommy, I might never see you again, but want you to know I love you, terribly awfully, badly, missing your stories, understanding why you could never hold us or pick us up, but you baked a wicked Chocolate Pudding Fudge Cake in that pan got the handles burned off. I can see your Ping Pong paddle, the bell in kindergarten, the accordion by the Three Trees down by Blanco Canyon, and I don't know why now, but lost sheep never don't get not found, eventually, as Split Ear could tell you, knobs of shiny hands on the reins of her kneel-down horse, like the horse, Brownie?, brought you, Renelda, Eleanor and your twin brother, Uncle Harold, back home in a blizzard, yeah?-

-hold my hands-

And never, never, never let go.
Hold on.

-Hold on-

-Hold on. Hold on. Hold on. Hold on-

Sacred Painting in the Ground

You came to my place from a long way cold
      and windy. You are eminent. You slept here.

I have no clothes; my feathers are plucked. You watch
me
slumped, fat, battered, queasy in the middle of the blessing, as hefty
           guardians invested in many colors
    bend down, down through the narrow dawn
door.

Forgive me. I do not honor all you. I do not honor
      you who bring from a height the eagle flight,
in medicine palms of pollen. I honor
      the old snake, the laughing kind one, dripping
  venom and happiness
in his battered embrace. Who likes me,
me, the scruffy white crow they threw out the back,
      can't fly, can't feed her children, can't sing,
  comforted in days without a country, of talk and
wait.

Endless storytelling, the children rustling, the people zooming restless gloom.
          Our feathers flutter; the whole world
complete in herbs on earth, smeared, corrupted, dances,
heals.
   Plucked, cracked and crooked in standing, you came in the blustering, guttural
beginning chanting
    as the last chant the song the end again. Tomorrow we fly home.
Tomorrow, you may sweep up the shattered rainbows
      replanted in your sacred pocket. Beauty being again
        finished.

Snow Dancing with the Aurium

"There are no buckets."

We tease a tickle,

trickle of crystal; jeeze,

last time this happened,

thinking I am melting, melting, not-

only-lonely,

droplet

on the edge running away down to actual Bigger

swell wave force curve of mass to crash

lively lace sliding back

to the bottom of the "well,"

that decline, last time, roadtrip freezer to tears

thawed and fallen,

we had no flaw, no memory

in alimentary serpentine

canaling, rock candy sugar

strike years to wander to wider

minute mirrors of hazel

muddying round hours up the scream pipe to

emerald ephemeral foam to fade to black evaporation.

But glad, we're cycling around back up

the spiral thermal do over,

not knowing any wilder really how to snowcarve curves

but how it feels in a

snowflake

to finely

fall.

Snow dancing with the aurium of the falls.

Robert Sapolsky, 1. Introduction to Human Behavioral Biology – https://m.youtube.com/watch?v=NNnIGh9g6fA

How I Think Part of My Story Goes

Intentional Community Without Network

I was raised in a tiny intentional community 160 miles from the nearest social worker, about 11,000 miles from sanity. I know about cults. How could I advocate for networks of tiny intentional villages to restore sanity in Los Angeles? I can only say, just as bodies can achieve keen senses, villages can be open, unwalled, watched by loving eyes. I have experienced neurodiversity, bullying, exclusion and isolation. I've spent a lot of my life on fire. And I have come to know friendship, forgiveness, competence and community. It is sweet as poetry.

At 63, I guess I've eaten so much crow now I got soggy pinfeathers sticking out at odd places and times. You'd think I liked raw crow from the greasy bones leftover on the plate. I have been told by myself to shut up, shut up, shut up. Like that story of Quincy Jones when his broke lost mother finally came to see him perform in a jazz concert. She heckled him that everything he played was of the devil and the more he got heard the more damage he'd do.

When I was a kid I had this idea that I was poison, a little red devil. Red was my favorite color and the little kids bullied me, because I was white, because I wanted to be Diné; I remember sitting in a crib between the missionary apartment and the dorm of Navajo girls watching big people walk by, but nobody seemed to want to touch me until I was three when the girls started taking me to sex in the outhouse, which was heaven and hell. I was a very bad girl who sometimes ran away from my sex ring of missionary kids and sometimes ran to get it going.

Hell and heaven dwelt in my soul and muscle; I had a little friend rolled in a campfire by an alcoholic uncle; I should have saved him, white little missionary kid busy playing in the bed-rooms while the Rez burned down in a desert. I don't still know if it's his face and screams I remember or my own.

Before I'd decided to become a missionary too, I saw somebody mighty unsteady hold a black metal revolver on my dad. Third time somebody'd done that. Why'd they want to kill my dad? He loved them. Didn't he? Didn't he? Or did he just love the violence of adventure gleam of the stories told of persecution later in upstanding fellowship halls with plates of china and aluminum with velvet? No. I knew him. He was much more complicated than that. Complicated compassion.

My broken Daddy was a good teacher; loved us; he talked his student easy until the kid fell drunk to the ground while my Mom ran around bandaging the blackened bloody baseball face of that man's friend. Blood and sacrifice all over the kitchen.

Neuroplasticity in Generational DNA

I remember another kid, my dad's student, killed on the highway, 17 years old, laid down on the black ice, drunk, ran over by a nice Italian tourist who came to the door in a panic screaming. Guess she wasn't used to it. The missionaries took two days building the casket laid out on a sawhorse in the mission laundry center. That pine cupboard never stopped to tower over my nine-year-old body until my eleventh final break-down at Bible College when my friend attempted suicide after Thanksgiving break, I guess, raped by her father again over the weekend. The shock was, rape could happen even to a white girl studying to be a wife of a pastor in a Bible School.

I'm no missionary now. Missionaries are omniscient and full of knowing everything. And I quit being activist long, long ago. I am a poet. I been told to take care of myself. First. But I did discover, it's a nice idea to put on your mask to breathe before you tend the baby, but really, when the pilot's flying DUI, you might get proactively creative.

Sometimes I'd like to apologize for being so free to squawk, to live substandard in LA. I've advocated non-suicide at Mayfield school for the rich in Pasadena for Painted Brain. I've read Ann Lamont on a hot bus bench, no trees and no bus, with a moneyman-educated man screaming stink and pain and cuss words at nobody who is his tribe. And yeah, we lost our way. It ain't about the food bank or the image on your taxes. It's about the Word.

It's simpler. Love. I found poetry. Mary Oliver, V. Kali, Lucy Tapahonso and Alex Petunia. I found the music in the conversation of yellow meadowlarks and flight of graphics in pigeon design.

Finding Myself in the Gray Bark Clack of Juniper Boughs

Now, somebody's going to say, "Well, Engleman writes poems characteristic of her 'bi' 'polar' 'dis' 'order.'" Nonsense. Even if the disputed "science" of psychiatry were socially empirical, the treatment is not. In the first place, any human being born with a genetic proclivity toward light, color, form, or music will become emotionally dysregulated when subjected to years of unmitigated violence. Sure, brain scans change; so does behavior. In light of scientific evidence of generational trauma, violence is not exclusively physical. Long-term virtual, nutritional and psychological violence can have the effect of life suppression, an eclectic link between the electric brain, the imagination and behavior. It's an illness outside in, and inside out. It's your unconscious genetics in action as much as mine.

Secondly, persons having gotten smart in endless research to survive the science of oppression, will be endlessly confused by a society that cannot find the bliss in a concert of diversity.

And thirdly, a highly sensitive individual who is incessantly curious, and needs something to do, as an Arabian pony needs to run and a German Shepherd needs to rescue, will become brought to paralysis through years of physical emotional suppression. Lies. All three, the poet, the horse and the dog, will die in a cage or lie down, beaten out of her nature. When hope or joy finally comes, the creative individual is sprung, bursting like a worried yeller zit on the "doctor's" nose. My every "episode" was immediately preceded by either violence or hope. The balance of the light sword must be taught to a brain through the body, not in a chair. Temperance is a fruit of the Spirit.

The synesthesia in the performance of poetry, whether in print or spoken word, brings us back to the center where we should have been before it all began. Drugs are the last thing young people need to return to homes of hope, through loving coaching in meditative physical movement and vocational skills. The current practice in our 'hospitals' of bullying a 'patient' to violence in order to force psychotropics must end, along with sending young men of color to jail in consequence of this practice. Neglected too long, anxiety, rage and fear become treatment resistant. By now, we all may need sedation and restraint.

In blindly following the mumbling of pop EuroAmerican eugenics, the united States mental health system has done tremendous disservice and damage to our people, particularly toward cultures, languages and physical operating systems that are simply dismissed as irrelevant by grants recipients or pop psychologists with car payments. You cannot do psychotherapy in a second language or social work on paper. Generational trauma is scientific, but genetic resilience is not static; it is dynamic. Mass mental illness in a "first world" is as much about money as patience. Didn't Jesus go a bit mad with the money changers?

Turmoil in the High C's

I hear voices all right, as did Jesus Christ in Gethsemane and John McCain in residence at the Hanoi Hilton. I listen: Grand-mothers, angels, kids in middle school, Stella Cruz, Allah and Pema Chodron on a cell phone.

And now, when I tell you, "Don't do it," Don't Do It. Do not die young or too early old. Your life is the treasure you're hunting. You have got to feel just once the blessing and the power, surviving, when you've been spit up by the whale on a California Beach. I have been spat up from the belly of that fish so many times, you can't tell my skin from the seaweed. And you cannot ever believe hope and love, until you've flapped your natural shady eagle flimsy feathers accidentally too high sky-high out over the city, screaming "Whee! Wha!? Wha?! Wha!? Wha?! What in the world am I doing HERE?!!!!!"

I've flown flocks, fog and sleet, but I've also flown the sunrise, the grass and the bougainvillea, high over Hollywood, hung out in the Arts District, or on a bus flight across Pasadena Suicide Bridge where I lost my friend to cop care. I've floated free out over the clouds to Christmas to Bozana Belokosa's candy yams and collard greens and whiskey. You can't tell me shut up now, I been born.

Intention and Definition of the Audience

My writing is for anyone who is different from anyone else, as are we all. If I blearily drove with a license and got a real job, that'd be enough for some. But if I was heard, writing in the exclusive language of the British Empire, having had my ancestral languages choked from my education, my blessing would be enough. If I could cut off my skin and turn it inside out, my life would be enough, in contrition as a citizen of these united States, having witnessed the results of democracy meted out by force and whitewash.

I'm a traveler who has forgotten her language and gender, a woman abandoned by some, but with friends, and the animals and characters living in my house and in my mind. I'd like a run through the fissures in Tanzania with my forgotten grandmothers, a stroll through Paris with the dead poets, leaving my Teutonic ancestors buried in a bunker. I would swaddle my vets and foster kids on handmade cradleboards of the Diné and the Sami.

I'd like to find the Blackfeet who lost my Dad's mom, and the German farmer who lost my Mom's mom. I would bring this healing of difference to my vast community of friends. I write as an immigrant who has no country, and no understanding, lost. And found. I kneel in gratefulness to the One Global Creator. I wear the scars of freedom. And this is, simply, that I cannot be followed, but only seen from a distance, as can anyone else. This is what we have in common. That is my word.

Populated Gratefulness

I am grateful for my life. Whether or not I adequately reflect the mercy:

- All the clouds, auriums, and poems I do not mention, being too frail and too small to hold you all together in a book.
- Sandra Goodwick, my intentional sister, fellow survivor, mentor in animate Kintsugi collage
- My poetry grandmother, Kathabela Wilson, for her kind haiku and living poetry
- Hiram Sims for his leadership, courage, and competent compassion. And for the community at Sims Library of Poetry and the Community Literature Initiative throughout the world
- Alex Petunia, *Tending My Wild*, for gentility in the facilitation of healthy activism
- Karo Ska, *Loving My Salt-Drenched Bones*, a fire, courage, and clarity that keep me on
- Cory Cofer, *Dreaming Under Polka-Dot Stars*, for living the proactive adventure of revolutionary change through storytelling in gatherings, and in empowering us all

My CLI Book Production Team for their graciousness in reworking the complications of my vision in a short time.

- Krystle May Statler, CLI Book Production Manager, for patient clarifying nudge
- Emily Anne Evans, Second Book Production Manager, for elegant smoozhe of my amateur bumpy terror and reluctance to sprout some
- Megan Duncan, for her encouragement and for actually listening to the audio, the music, in my compositions of conversation
- Heidi Unkefer, my cover designer, for an album cover in Art Deco to reflect feminine courage and the wonder of winter and infancy as part of many seasons

- Mary Flylypowycz, for these years of depth therapy in storytelling and healing touch
- Fred Sugerman, Medicine Dance, for settling me into the rhythm of life through stillness, breath, dance, art, meditation, creativity, storytelling and body movement in poetry

- Colleen Sugerman, the performance art of holding the community of dance in grace, power and fluidity
- Pro Peers ENTRY NETWORK, Becky Lewis, Dana Dunlap and Marie Kenfak for friendship and stability
- Heart Forward LA, Kerry Morrison and Evangeline Lee, for shaking up the box with wings, rails, tires and boots
- My family, Timothy Foster, Jeanne Huntley, and Trasi Platero, for walking me through the first part of my life.
- Kathy Foster, for listening patiently and kindly to my occasional rants
- Lennie Moore, for partnering through twelve years of rehab
- Stella Cruz, Medicine Pathways, for meditative presence online for months
- Yvonne Sandoval, for her healing and redemption in crystal light
- Esther Perez, for nonjudgmental analysis in listening friendship
- Brent Popham, for consistent demonstration of proactive compassion
- Chelle Thomas, for her passion for Epiphany Village, the Clubhouse, the Co-Housing and the Retreat Center. It will build!
- Jacquelyn Labrie, for relentless optimism and grace
- Miguel Riveras, for restoring our broken villages through drumming, sacred silence and poetry, and for giving me the beautiful words of Humberto Aka'bal
- The Unitarian Universalist Fellowship of the Olympic Peninsula - Lynn Unger, Bruce Bode, Jamal Rahman, Harmony Rutter, and Joseph Bednarik - for leading me tenderly to water through scriptures, children's stories, poetry, parables and music
- PATH, for building the house in which to nurture the home
- All Saints Writers Group for getting me to the start gate.
- Pat Collins, for horizon in crossing the great water, Irish nobility in a new world
- Project Return Peer Support Network: Jason Garcia, Ashley Flores and Jessica Oyerzides for evidence of the efficacy of experience and respite.

9 798218 370831